ANIMAL TRACKS AND SIGNS OF
NORTH AMERICA

ANIMAL TRACKS AND SIGNS OF NORTH AMERICA

Richard P. Smith

STACKPOLE BOOKS

Published by
STACKPOLE BOOKS
5067 Ritter Road
Mechanicsburg, PA 17055

Cover photograph by Richard P. Smith

Printed in the U.S.A.

Library of Congress Cataloging in Publication Data

Smith, Richard P, 1949–
    Animal tracks and signs of North America.

    Bibliography: p.
    Includes index.
    1. Animal tracks—North America.   I. Title.
QL768.S63   1982   599   82-10561
ISBN O-8117-2124-8 (pbk.)

Dedication
To some of the important women in my life: my wife Lucy who takes care of the important details of running a household while I'm tracking wildlife; my mother and two sisters, Kathy and Linda, who all encouraged my interest in wildlife and writing.

About the Author
Richard P. Smith is a free-lance outdoor writer and photographer who publishes regularly in such periodicals as *Outdoor Life*, *Sports Afield*, and *Field & Stream*. *Fins and Feathers*, *Deer and Deer Hunting*, and *Michigan Sportsman* also claim him as a field editor. In his "spare time" he writes a monthly column for *Michigan-Out-of-Doors* and *Great Lakes Fisherman*.

Contents

Acknowledgments

THERE ARE A lot of people I would like to thank for helping to make this book possible. First on the list are my Dad, who introduced me to the outdoors, and Uncle George, who started my interest in tracks and taught me how to read and follow them.

I also want to thank Ken Lowe, Bob Skuggen, and Dave Richey, among others, without whose help and encouragement my writing career may not have advanced enough to make writing a book such as this possible.

Other photographers were also very helpful in completing this book. They include Chuck Adams, Kent and Donna Dannon, Karl Maslowski, Leonard Lee Rue Enterprises, Scot Stewart, Frank Martin, Lloyd Bare, Ed Erickson III, Jim Hammill, Jeff Bunker, Jim Haveman, and Sue Adams.

State and federal agencies helped in obtaining illustrations, too, such as the Michigan and Wisconsin Departments of Natural Resources, the New Mexico Department of Game and Fish, and the National Park Service. I would like to extend special thanks to Dick Lehman with the Michigan DNR, Jean Meyer with the Wisconsin DNR and Carol Maass with the National Park Service for their help in this endeavor.

Thanks also to those who have shared the trails of wildlife with me: Jim Haveman, Gene Ballew, my brother Bruce, and many more.

And finally, I would like to thank the people at Stackpole Books, especially Ruth Dennison-TeDesco, who felt from the start that I could produce a valuable reference on wildlife tracks and sign.

Preface

WILDLIFE HAVE BEEN important in my life, as I hope they will continue to be. I have been fortunate enough to spend more time than most people among them, simply enjoying their presence and beauty, photographing them or playing a role along with them in the natural scheme of things.

Actually observing wildlife is the greatest of thrills, but achieving this is not always possible. Therefore, I have learned to appreciate their tracks, sign, and sounds just as much. The ability to interpret these indications of their presence has often enabled me to eventually see the animals themselves. The words that fill the following pages were written in the hopes that others can profit from the information in the same way I have.

The many photos that complement the text are included for the same reason. One of the primary reasons that I started carrying a camera with me years ago was to better enable me to share some of the sights of the wild with others who were not or are not as fortunate as I have been. It is my hope that is accomplished through the pages of this book.

Introduction

I CRAMMED AS much information as possible in this book to make it a valuable reference for anyone interested in wildlife. Emphasis, of course, is on wildlife tracks. Therefore, the beginning of each chapter discusses the basic track pattern for the group of wildlife covered in those pages. More specifics about individual tracks of various species within that group are listed individually further on in the text.

In some cases, track patterns differ enough for each species in particular chapters that they are described separately.

For the most part, mammals discussed in chapters all belong to the same family such as weasels, squirrels, cats, canines, and bears. However, there is some variation from this, which will be noted in chapters on tree-dwelling animals other than squirrels and aquatic mammals. Rather than devote a separate chapter to opossums, for example, they are included together with raccoons, ringtails, coatis, and porcupines, the only common element being that they climb trees. It may not be scientific, but it makes sense to me.

Otters are actually members of the weasel family, but they are also aquatic, so they are considered in the same chapter with beaver, nutria, and muskrat. Pikas are normally considered with rabbits and hares, but I put them in the chapter on small mammals along with mice, voles, shrews, gophers, moles, and rats. Armadillos fall into the miscellaneous category with turtles, frogs, toads, snakes, and worms.

Since deer are one of the most popular and widespread forms of hooved wildlife, a single chapter is devoted to their tracks and sign. Other members of the deer family—elk, moose and caribou—are considered in the following chapter, and additional wildlife that have hooves come next.

Photos of as many wildlife tracks as possible are included in this book to better help identify those seen in the field, since actual footprints do not always resemble detailed sketches found in other guidebooks. Plus, photos of the wildlife themselves eliminate any doubt as to which species is being discussed.

After track sizes and shapes are explained, other pertinent sign such as scat, feeding activity, territorial markers, and more are described for each species. Scat descriptions are not included for all wildlife because in some cases it is simply not important or seldom seen. Here again, as many photos as possible are shown to help identify specific types of sign. Even without reading a word of the text, there is a lot to be learned about wildlife by simply looking at the photos and reading the corresponding captions.

Additional information included for each species of wildlife are coloration, markings, and sizes that can be helpful in identifying wildlife that is observed while afield. The photos of wildlife mentioned earlier will complement these descriptions. There are also brief descriptions of the habitat preferences and ranges of wildlife to give an idea where they themselves or their tracks are likely to be found.

One type of information not included in this book is scientific names of wildlife, not that I do not know them or could not find out what they were if I did not. I learned the Latin names for mammals in school, and I have not had the need to use them since, except when kiddingly trying to convince a friend that I saw the tracks of an exotic form of wildlife, when actually talking about a common species. If you need to know the scientific name of wildlife, there are plenty of other books you can refer to.

A couple of special chapters are devoted to sounds mammals and birds make. Other chapters discuss how to take good photos of wildlife tracks yourself or make plaster casts of them, plus how to age tracks and how to actually track wildlife. The final section of the book includes a fun quiz to test how much you have learned. If you read the preceding pages carefully, you are sure to score high. Good luck and have fun!

1

Squirrels

SQUIRRELS ARE HOPPERS like rabbits, but they normally leave two sets of paired tracks, one in front of the other, with prints from the larger hind feet appearing in front of smaller front feet. In tracks where the toes are visible, there will be five where hind feet landed and four toes in impressions left by forefeet. Rabbit and hare tracks show only four toes in prints from rear feet, when they are spread enough to register, and toes from front feet are rarely visible in tracks. The impressions left by front feet are usually offset from one another in rabbit tracks, too.

Not all members of the squirrel family are tree dwellers. Woodchucks, marmots, prairie dogs, ground squirrels, and gophers are closely related to tree squirrels, but have adapted for living in burrows underground. Some of them live in areas where there are few trees, but at least one of these members of the squirrel family—woodchucks—is sometimes found in wooded areas, and may climb trees on occasion to obtain food or sun itself.

Tracks that ground-dwelling members of the squirrel family make are different than those characteristic of squirrels because they walk rather than hop, although tracks of these animals are not often seen, except at, or near burrow entrances in sand, dust, or snow. These animals hibernate during the winter though, so any prints they leave in the snow will be during early spring or late fall, and not far from their burrows.

Where their tracks are visible, hind feet show five toes and front, four. The long claws these animals use for digging often leave prominent marks. Feet are generally pointed straight ahead. When running, burrowing squirrels may leave a diagonal line of prints, or a track pattern similar to tree-dwelling squirrels, although both back and front feet may be offset, showing one slightly ahead of its mate. In either case, the tracks should lead to a nearby burrow.

The primary species of tree-dwelling squirrels in North America are grays, reds, flying, and fox squirrels. Chipmunks also climb trees regularly and may live in them on occasion, but usually occupy burrows. Tracks of the various species can generally be differentiated by the length of hind feet.

Chipmunks

The prints of chipmunks measure from 1⅛ to 1½ inches in length. Lengths of 1¾ inches or more are average for red or pine squirrels, with the prints of flying squirrels averaging slightly shorter. Flying squirrel tracks may also start some distance from a tree where a skid mark of sorts will appear where the animal landed. Red squirrel tracks seldom start more than a foot from the base of a tree. The norm for back feet of gray squirrels is 2¼ to 2½ inches, and the larger fox squirrels have feet that are from 2¾ to 3 inches long. Tracks from these animals can be seen in the snow during fall, winter, and spring when they venture forth to feed, usually on sunny days.

Chipmunks have black and white lines that run along their sides and around the eyes, with most of their body being various shades of brown. The only squirrel they can be confused with is the golden-mantled variety found in some western states. These chipmunklike squirrels do not have white or black lines around their eyes. The weight of chipmunks is measured in ounces.

Tree-Dwelling Squirrels

Flying squirrels are not large either and are gray in color with loose folds of skin extending between front and back legs. Their large eyes are a clue they are primarily nocturnal. It is not unusual for these animals to make nightly visits to bird feeders during winter months. They sometimes take up residence in bird houses or nesting boxes.

Red and pine (also called chickaree) squirrels look a lot alike, being red or orange in color and weighing under a pound. Gray squirrels are most often gray in color, but black ones are not uncommon and white gray squirrels sometimes occur. These animals weigh around a pound. Fox squirrels weigh

Chipmunk filling cheek pouches with nuts from a picnic table.

Chipmunk tracks from display at Seney National Wildlife Refuge, Michigan. Notice five toes on hind feet and four on front feet.

CHIPMUNK (actual size)

Flying squirrel. (Photograph courtesy of Leonard Lee Rue III.)

Fox squirrels are the largest tree squirrels.

Look for nut shells on logs, stumps, and rocks, which squirrels use as dining tables, like this gray squirrel with an acorn.

in between 2 and 3 pounds, on the average, and are rusty gray to reddish in color.

Gray, fox, and flying squirrels are most often found in stands of hardwood trees, some of which produce nuts such as oaks, hickorys, and beeches. However, the animals do well on agricultural crops such as corn in farming areas where woodlots are available. Red and pine squirrels tend to occupy coniferous forests where they feed on seeds from pine cones, although they are found in hardwood forests, too.

The range of gray and fox squirrels roughly takes in the eastern half of the lower United States, although grays range as far north as southern Canada. The northern limit of the fox squirrel's range does not extend that far, nor does it include northeastern states such as Maine, Vermont, New Hampshire, New York, Massachusetts, Connecticut, and Rhode Island. A subspecies of gray squirrel is also found in states along the western coast and in Arizona.

Flying squirrels are distributed across the eastern half of the United States, all of Canada, into Alaska and south to some states in the northwestern part of the country. Red and pine squirrels range over most of the northern half of the United States where the habitat is suitable, and in mountainous regions of the west, all across Canada, and into Alaska.

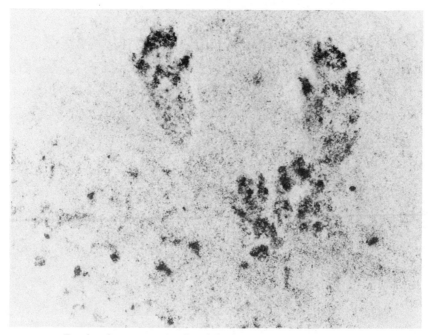

Tracks of a gray squirrel with both front and rear feet paired.

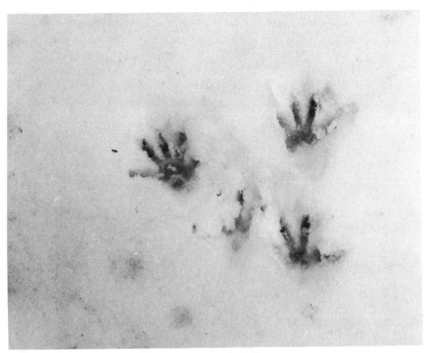

Red squirrel track.

Huge pile of pine cone scales here pinpoints a red squirrel's favored feeding area or kitchen. (Photograph courtesy of Kent and Donna Dannen.)

Other than tracks, signs of their feeding activity are good clues to squirrels' presence. Nutshells that gray or fox squirrels have broken open can usually be found on stumps, rocks, or logs that serve as dining tables. Corn cobs stripped of their kernels in woodlots near cornfields are usually left by fox squirrels. Red squirrels regularly leave piles of pine cone scales where they have picked them apart for the seeds. A photo in this chapter shows an exceptionally large pile of cone scales in a red squirrel's "kitchen." All of the tree squirrels dig in leaves or snow to salvage stored food. Leaves are generally visible on top of the snow at these locations.

These squirrels make nests of leaves, twigs, and other materials that are another sign to look for. The material is most often packed into a crotch formed between a limb and the tree trunk. Nests are often circular in shape and are most noticeable after the leaves fall in the autumn. Squirrels also live in hollow tree cavities.

Ground-Dwelling Species

Tracks of ground-dwelling members of the squirrel family are not as valuable as signs of their presence as burrows are. The location of prairie dogs, for example, is best determined by spotting concentrations of their

A squirrel nest made of leaves. Nests of this type are often abundant in areas where there are a lot of squirrels.

Woodchucks live in woodpiles and rockpiles in addition to burrows in fields.

burrows with mini, volcano-shaped entrances on open grasslands or semi-arid plains. Prairie dogs are sociable animals, so where there is one, there is usually more. Burrows are normally close together.

Woodchuck or groundhog holes are marked by piles of fresh soil at their entrance, which is deposited on one side rather than being distributed around the opening. Piles of dirt excavated by woodchucks contrast sharply with the green grass of fields where they are usually located and can be spotted from a distance. These animals are also at home in piles of rock and wood. I have seen a number of woodchucks that took up residence under bridges over rivers and streams.

Marmots are the woodchuck's western counterpart. Their burrows are similar to those used by 'chucks when in fields. However, they commonly dig burrows under rocks where they sometimes are hard to see. Both woodchucks and marmots may have one or more exit holes that are less conspicuous than the main entrance.

There are a number of species of ground squirrels in North America such as spotted, thirteen-lined, California, Columbian, Franklin, and Arctic varieties. Their tunnels have narrow entrances and may or may not have accumulations of dirt there. Most of the ones I have seen do not.

Gophers spend most of their time underground where they feed on roots

Walking tracks of a woodchuck in the snow.

Running track of a woodchuck. Notice how similar this pattern is to that of tree squirrels.

A thirteen-lined ground squirrel, one of several varieties found in North America.

A pair of prairie dogs on a characteristically shaped burrow entrance.

and tubers, but they do eat grass and other vegetation above ground, too. Gophers were common on a golf course I frequented as a boy in California, where they were considered pests. Gopher burrows are marked by mounds of soil that may be fan shaped, with the entrance hole on one edge of the pile usually plugged with dirt. The animals keep the entrances filled in, except when new burrows are under construction to push the dirt out, and when feeding above ground.

Small ridges of soil about 2 inches in diameter on the ground mark the former locations of gopher tunnels under the snow. The corridors through the snow are lined with dirt when in use, which is deposited in ridges when the snow melts. These dirt ridges do not have tunnels under them like those of moles and are usually smaller. Raised soil that marks mole tunnels may measure at least 3 inches high and 6 inches in diameter.

There are a number of varieties of pocket gophers, which are distributed throughout the western two-thirds of the United States, into Canada and a few southeastern states such as Florida, Georgia, and Alabama. These animals have small ears, prominent front teeth (incisors) for gnawing, and long claws on front feet for digging. Their tails do not have hair on them. Gophers vary in color from yellow to brown, with color mutations not uncommon. They occupy open areas such as pastures, golf courses, and agricultural areas.

Ground squirrels are gray to brown in color with shorter tails than tree squirrels. Several varieties are spotted, and one species common in the midwest has stripes down its back. Ground squirrels of one species or another are found in most of the western United States, much of the midwest, in parts of Canada and most of Alaska.

Marmots (also called rockchucks) and woodchucks resemble one another with chunky bodies and short legs. Their weights range from less than 10 pounds to more than 15. Most of the animals are shades of brown, but they can be yellowish, gray like the hoary marmot, or almost black. Marmots range from Alaska southward to Arizona and New Mexico, being most common in the mountains. Woodchucks are concentrated in the northeast and midwest, but are also at home in some southern states. They are common in Canada and their range extends into Alaska. Some of the greatest concentrations of woodchucks I have seen were in Ontario.

Most *prairie dogs* are tan to brown in color, but I have seen white ones in South Dakota's Badlands, and they are about a third to one-half the size of woodchucks. Their range includes a band of states from Mexico to Canada including some states in both the midwest and west. Prairie dogs inhabit prairie regions (hence their name), where grass and other vegetation provide food.

2

More Tree Dwellers

THE THREE MAJOR mammals discussed in this chapter—raccoons, porcupines, and opossums—have an adaptation for living in trees in common, but their individual tracks do not resemble one another, and so they will be described separately.

Raccoons, Coatis, and Ringtails

Raccoons, for instance, have five toes on each foot, which are generally visible in tracks. When they walk, imprints from the left hind foot are usually next to right front footprints. The right hind foot and left front are usually paired.

Hind feet leave tracks longer than front feet. Front footprints look more like hands than feet with characteristically long, fingerlike toes. In fact, raccoons use their front feet just like hands when searching for food. Raccoons are often associated with water in rivers, streams, lakes, ponds, and marshes where they feed on mussels, crayfish, fish, and frogs. Look for their tracks in mud or sand at these locations. An accumulation of empty mussel shells on banks is a sure sign of a favored raccoon feeding spot.

A raccoon.

'Coons will also range into upland areas with nut- or fruit-bearing trees for them to feed on. Their taste for corn is well known. Hollow cavities in hardwood trees are sought by the animals for winter dens, daytime resting spots and places to raise their young. Burrows are used in areas where trees are absent or small. Mating takes place during late winter and spring, so it is not unusual to see the tracks of a male searching for a mate in the snow.

Raccoons have distinctive ringed tails and eyes masked in black. Two relatives of the raccoon that have similar markings are the coati and ringtail. The coati's face is mostly masked in black, except for the long snout. Coatis have longer, slimmer tails than 'coons with light rings that may not be visible on some animals. Ringtails are catlike in appearance, but have pointed snouts

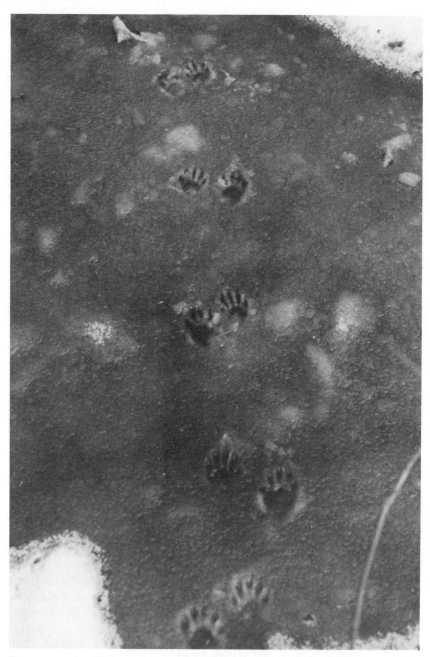

Raccoon tracks. Notice pairing of opposing front and rear feet, with long toes on front feet.

A group of coati. (Photograph courtesy of Kent and Donna Dannen.)

Ringtail. (Photograph courtesy of Irene Vandermolen.)

and short legs. These animals also have longer tails than raccoons with prominent dark bands around them, as well as at the tip. They do not have any black on their faces though. Coatis and ringtails are as adept at tree climbing as raccoons.

Raccoons range in weight from 10 to more than 30 pounds, and coatis are similar in size with larger animals weighing less than 30 pounds. Most ringtails weigh between 2 and 3 pounds.

Tracks of the coati have five toes fore and aft, but the toes are not long and fingerlike as the raccoons are. As a result, coati tracks are shorter, measuring 1½ to 1¾ inches for front feet and up to 3 inches for hind feet. Front feet of 'coons leave prints between 2 and 3 inches long and hind feet are more than 3 inches in length.

Ringtail tracks resemble those of house cats, only they exhibit five toes rather than four. Marks from toenails may or may not show in tracks since they are semi-retractable. Tracks from both front and back feet are close in size. These animals are nocturnal, more so than raccoons, seldom venturing from cover during hours of daylight. Their large eyes are well suited for seeing at night.

Raccoons are distributed over much of the lower United States and a large portion of southern Canada. Coatis and ringtails are concentrated in the southwest. Parts of Texas, Arizona, and New Mexico and most of Mexico

Raccoon scat.

Opossum. (Photograph courtesy of Karl Maslowski.)

are home for the coati. Ringtails range from Texas, Oklahoma, and Kansas westward to California and the southwest corner of Oregon. They are also well established in Mexico.

Droppings from raccoons that I have seen in stands of oaks were uniform in diameter, ropelike in appearance and 3 to 6 inches long, although they are sometimes broken in pieces. 'Coons that have been feeding on acorns leave scats that are gray to brown in color. Those feeding on fruits or berries are black to brown with seeds usually visible. 'Coons feeding in the water leave looser droppings that fall apart. Remains of crayfish may be visible in them. Accumulations of droppings sometimes occur at the base of trees raccoons den in.

Scats from coati and ringtails are similar, although ringtail droppings tend to be smaller in diameter. Ringtails regularly defecate on top of rocks. Raccoons have the same habit, which is carried over to logs as well.

Opossums

Opossums have five toes per foot like raccoons, but toes on hind feet have a unique arrangement. A distinct, clawless thumb is offset from the other toes, and usually points off to the side or backward at an angle, while the other toes (the three middle ones together and the outside one separate) face forward. Tracks of front feet resemble small hands, but toes are not as long as those of raccoons, measuring about 1½ inches long. Front and rear tracks from opposite sides of the body are usually paired, and drag marks from the tail sometimes register in the snow.

These animals are white to gray in color with hairless ears and ratlike tails. Their tails aid in climbing. Another unique feature about opossums is they are the only marsupials in North America. That is, females have an abdominal pouch where they nurse their helpless young until they grow hair and are large enough to move about on their own. Even then, young opossums hitch rides on their mother's back at times. Adults may weigh between four and eight pounds, with some big males being heavier.

Opossums frequent areas with water and visit fruit-bearing trees like raccoons. Their diets are also similar. The animals are primarily nocturnal and will use dens in trees. Their range includes most of the eastern, southern, and midwestern United States, except Maine and the northern portions of Michigan, Wisconsin, and Minnesota. Opossums are found in parts of California, Oregon, Washington, Arizona, and New Mexico, too.

Porcupines

Porcupines walk pigeon-toed with footprints pointed inward. Both feet have large, oval-shaped pads that are slightly larger on back feet. Front feet have four toes, with an extra one present on each of the hind feet. Imprints of the rough surface of pads are sometimes visible in tracks. Drag marks from feet and tail may be visible in the snow. Tail drags are sometimes visible in sand. In deep, soft snow, porkies leave furrows where they walk.

The appearance of these quill-covered animals should be familiar to most people. They are generally black in color, with white on quills, and can weigh up to 30 pounds or more, but the average is probably somewhere around 15 pounds. Porkies are most often found in wooded areas, but I have seen them above timberline in the Rockies and far out in grassy fields where their armor would protect them from most predators. Fishers are the only animal known to prey on porcupines with consistent success, although bobcats succeed in killing them occasionally.

Porcupines are not the favorite animal of lumbermen due to their habit of gnawing bark from trees to eat, sometimes removing bark completely from

Opossum track. Front and rear feet from opposing sides leave prints next to each other like the raccoon. (Photograph courtesy of Leonard Lee Rue III.)

Distinctive hind foot of an opossum with offset, nailless thumb.

Porcupine climbing a tree.

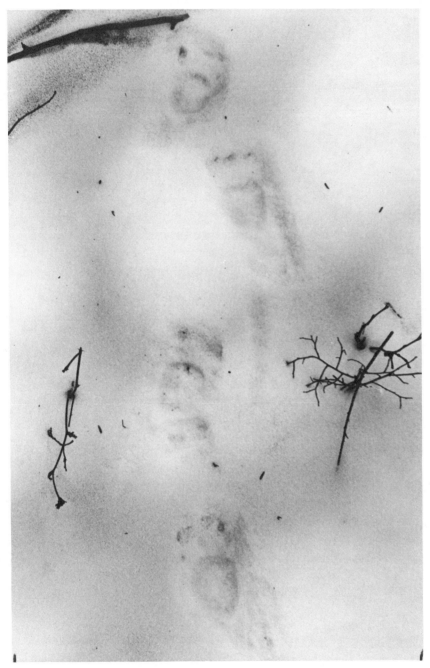

Porcupine tracks. Notice how prints are pointed inward.

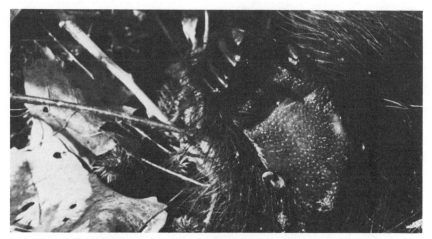

Hind foot of a porcupine. Rough surface sometimes shows in tracks.

A porcupine gnawed the bark around the base of tree in the foreground, killing it. Another damaged tree is in the background.

This hollow stump was occupied for some time by a porcupine, obvious by the accumulation of droppings.

around tree trunks, which kills the trees. Trees with large patches of missing bark on limbs and trunk are obvious porky signs. Hemlock and white cedar are favored winter foods. Snow that is littered with small pieces of hemlock or cedar under one of these trees is an indication of a porcupine dining above. I have seen porkies break off aspen branches in the spring and eat the buds and eat leaves from aspen saplings in the summer. Droppings and urine-stained snow will usually be present at the base of trees occupied by porcupines.

Their scat is in pellet form that resemble those of deer in shape, although porky pellets are longer. They are brown in color, too, as opposed to deer pellets that are more often black, at least when fresh. Den sites used by porcupines in hollow stumps or trees usually have large accumulations of pellets present.

Porcupines range across the entire western United States, the upper Great Lakes and northeast states, all of Canada, and most of Alaska. These animals are sluggish enough that they can be killed with a club, if a person becomes lost and is desperate for food.

3

Weasel Family

MOST MEMBERS OF the weasel family have a distinctive track pattern in the snow, which is the medium their prints are most often visible in. More often than not, their tracks consist of two depressions side by side. Weasels themselves, plus many of their relatives, are bounders and when more than a skiff of snow is present on the ground, their front and back feet leave impressions one on top of the other, or practically so.

Prints of all four feet will sometimes be visible in wet snow, and the pattern will resemble those of tree squirrels. However, the feet of members of the weasel family are not as consistently paired as those of squirrels, and there are five toes on each of the weasel's feet, although all of the toes are seldom visible in the prints of weasels themselves, as opposed to four visible toes in front footprints of squirrels. Some members of the weasel family climb trees like squirrels, so that trait alone is not always reliable in differentiating between tracks of the two families.

Members of the weasel family regularly travel underneath the snow's surface, as well as on top, when it is deep and fluffy. Tracks on the snow may suddenly disappear and reappear some distance away. This past winter I noticed some weasel tracks that could be puzzling to individuals not familiar with this habit. The animal would come up from under the snow and make one bound, then disappear under the snow again for a matter of feet, reappear and make another bound, then dive into the snow again.

The two prints left on the snow's surface were connected by drag marks from the animal's feet. It appeared as though the animal was finding travel easier under the snow than on top because of the lack of support on the snow's surface.

In mud or a skiff of snow, the track pattern spreads out into a diagonal string of four individual footprints. The above information applies to long and shorttail weasels, mink, pine martens, and fishers. Other members of the tribe, including skunks, badgers, and wolverines, are walkers, too, and leave correspondingly different track patterns. Skunks and badgers are not suited for tree climbing either. Since tracks differ among wolverines, skunks, and badgers, their characteristics will be discussed individually further on in this chapter. Otters are also members of the weasel family, but are discussed in the chapter on aquatic mammals.

Longtail and Shorttail Weasels

Tracks of the feet of longtail and shorttail weasels are less than an inch in length, as a rule. The animals have long, slender bodies that are brown with white extending from the chin all the way along the underside during

A long-tailed weasel in winter coat.

Track of a long-tailed weasel in deep, soft snow where the animal spent more time under the snow than on top of it.

spring and summer months. Weasels turn all white with the exception of a black-tipped tail during late fall and remain that color during the winter, except in locations where snow is uncommon. Weasels stay brown all year in snowless regions. White weasels are sometimes referred to as ermine, especially the shorttail.

Weasels are both curious and bold, at least longtails are, which is the variety I have had the most experience with. They feed on small mammals such as mice primarily, but occasionally kill a rabbit or hare. When observing weasels I sometimes make a squeak with my mouth like a mouse would and have had them come right up to me to investigate. If meat is placed before them or a hole they have recently entered, the animals often reappear to eat it or drag it off with a person standing only a matter of feet away.

On one occasion during the winter, I saw a longtail dash across a road nearby, and I quickly went after it hoping to photograph the animal. Since the animal was out of sight in seconds, I followed its tracks in the snow and was surprised to find them end abruptly at the base of a tree. At the time, I was not aware that weasels climb trees, so I was surprised to see the animal perched on a limb in the jack pine tree above me.

Weasels occupy a wide variety of habitat and can be seen almost anywhere in woodlands, brush, wetlands, rocks, and fields. I have seen them above timberline in the Rockies and in an open field in Montana where the animal had a den under a boulder, as well as in swamps and forests. The longtail ranges over most of the lower forty-eight states and well into Canada. About the only state in the lower United States where the weasel is absent is Oklahoma. They are also not normally found in northern Texas, most of Arizona and Utah, and parts of southern Nevada and California. Shorttails are distributed over most of Canada and all of Alaska, the Great Lakes states, the northeastern United States, and roughly the northern two-thirds of the western United States.

Mink

Mink are nothing more than a large weasel, weighing between 1 and 3 pounds. Large weasels may weigh half a pound, but are generally lighter. Mink and their tracks are closely associated with water—streams, rivers, lakes, and ponds—where their footprints can be seen in mud along banks or shoreline. Mink tracks usually measure just over an inch from their five toenails to heel.

These animals are brown in color year-round, not turning white like the weasel in the northern part of its range. They do have a spot of white on their chins, but this coloration does not extend down the chest and along the underside like weasels.

Mink feeding on a fish head. (Photograph courtesy of National Park Service.)

Hind feet of a mink. (Photograph courtesy of Wisconsin Department of Natural Resources.)

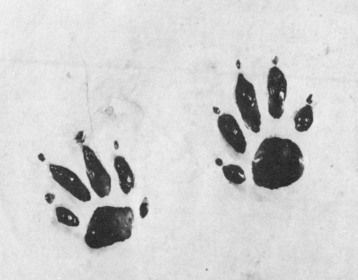

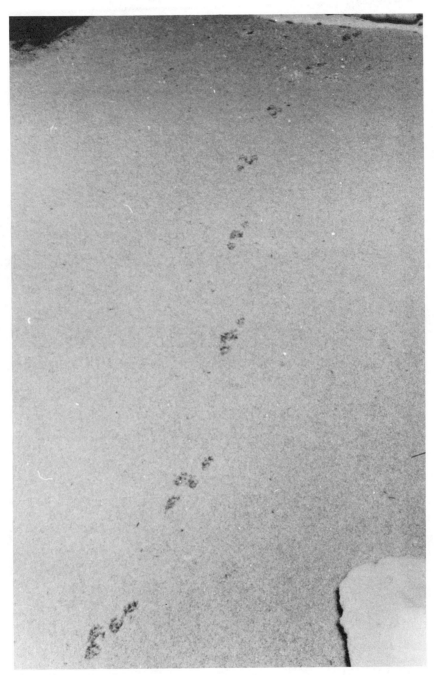

Track pattern of a mink in a skiff of snow.

In deeper snow, both weasels and mink leave two impressions side by side. This track following a stream was made by a mink.

Pine marten in a tree.

Mink are at home in the water and are excellent swimmers. Their prey consist of fish, muskrats, frogs, and other aquatic creatures, plus small land mammals, birds, and insects. Scats are not an important sign. The animals are distributed across North America, with the exception of northern-most Canada and Alaska, plus a band of states in the southwestern United States where water is scarce.

Pine Martens

Pine martens are similar in size to mink, but average a little larger, between 2 and 4 pounds. The hind feet of martens are about 1½ inches in length, but may leave prints 2 inches or more in the snow. Only four of five toes on feet usually register in tracks when they are visible at all. Marten tracks may be found near water like those of mink, but the animals do not usually spend as much time directly associated with water and do not often actually go in.

The body of these animals is brown in color, usually lighter than mink, with an even lighter colored face that appears tan. Martens have a throat patch that varies in color, but in many cases is yellow to orange. Trees play a major role in the pine marten's life, generally more so than other members of the weasel family discussed thus far. They prey on squirrels and birds in trees, as well as occupying cavities in them. Small mammals, including hares, make up the bulk of the marten's diet.

I saw a marten in a tree in Ontario last fall that I detected when hearing a low growllike noise it made. The animal jumped from tree to tree via limbs in much the same manner squirrels do. Most of Canada and Alaska is home to the pine marten. They also reside in the Great Lakes region, the northeast,

Pine marten tracks. (Photograph courtesy of Kent and Donna Dannen.)

and mountainous regions of the west in the lower United States. Martens have been transplanted from Canada to various states, including Michigan and Wisconsin, in an effort to increase their numbers and range.

Fishers

Fishers leave prints which show all five toes. Tracks of hind feet measure from 2 inches to more than twice that in the snow. Presence of five toes and toenails are usually enough to distinguish their tracks from those of bobcats and fox or coyote. Fishers sometimes walk in addition to bounding like other weasels.

The animals weigh from 4½ to 10 pounds, on the average. They are dark brown in color with long tails, but may appear black in color. Like the marten, the face is lighter than the body. And also like their close relative, fishers spend time in trees, sometimes jumping from one to another. Fishers are known for their ability to kill and eat porcupines without being injured by quills, although they feed on other mammals and birds, too.

The only live fishers I have seen at this point were captive animals studied by researcher Roger Powell in upper Michigan. One time while I was visiting Powell, he let the female, then the male out of their cages individually. When the male was free, he immediately came up to me, climbed my pantlegs and clamped my right wrist between its jaws in an apparent show of dominance. The animal did not bite down, so no damage was done. Rather than aggravate the situation, I remained motionless while Roger pried the fisher's jaws open.

Fishers are presently on the increase in my home region of Michigan's Upper Peninsula and neighboring northern Wisconsin where I hope to see a fisher in the wild someday. The animals are also found in northern Minnesota, from northern New York to Maine, and parts of California, Oregon, Idaho, Montana, and Wyoming in the United States. Their primary range is from east to west across much of Canada in the northern forests they prefer.

Wolverines

Wolverine tracks measure 3½ to 5 inches in length, and can be confused with those of wolves. However, five distinct toes should show in wolverine tracks, whereas wolf prints have four, and foot pads are shaped differently between the two as well. Front feet of wolverines have small, oval-shaped heel pads separated from the main pad that may show in prints. Wolves have one main foot pad in addition to four toe pads. Wolverines both walk and bound and leave corresponding track patterns.

Fisher in a tree. (Photograph courtesy of Leonard Lee Rue III.)

Left front footprint of a fisher. Notice the five distinct toes. (Photograph courtesy of Wisconsin Department of Natural Resources.)

Fisher track with front and rear prints side by side. (Photograph courtesy of Scott Johnson.)

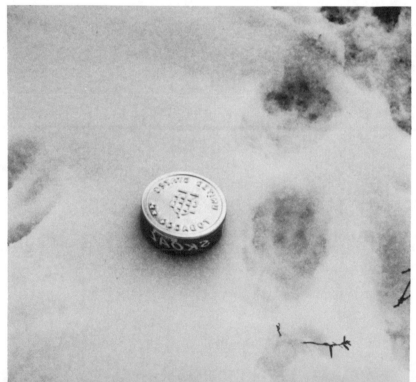

A wolverine raiding a cabin. (Photograph courtesy of Leonard Lee Rue III.)

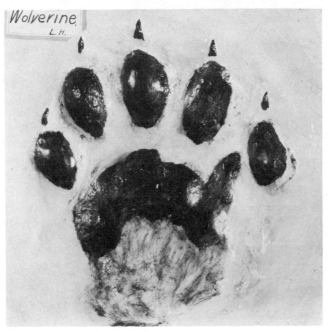

Wolverine track of a left hind foot. (Photograph courtesy of Wisconsin Department of Natural Resources.)

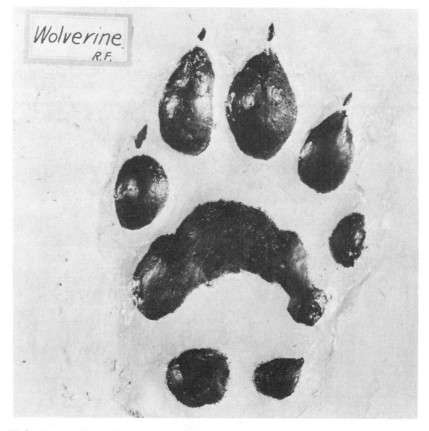

Wolverine track of a right front foot. (Photograph courtesy of Wisconsin Department of Natural Resources.)

The animals are brown in color, with contrasting stripes of light brown, yellow, or orange on sides of the body that join at the tail, and another band across the top of the head. Their tails are bushy and short in relation to the length of the body, although much longer than the tails of bears, which they resemble somewhat, depending on the angle and distance from which they are viewed. Wolverines weigh from 15 to 25 pounds, with both lighter and heavier weights on record.

Wolverines occupy open terrain such as the tundra and mountain regions above timberline, although they do enter forests, too. Their primary range is northern Canada and Alaska, but they are found throughout British Columbia and range south from there into portions of the western United States. States where their presence has been recorded are Montana, Idaho, Washington, Wyoming, Colorado, Utah, California, and Oregon.

Badgers

Badgers are diggers like some members of the squirrel family, leaving tracks of front feet with noticeable claw marks. They walk somewhat pigeon-toed like the porcupine, but have five toes per foot, and shorter claws of hind feet do not normally show in prints. Porkies have four toes on front feet and claws register in prints of both front and back feet. Badger tracks are 3 to 3½ inches in length and lead to a burrow or will be found in sand where the animals are hunting.

Fairly large pieces of ground are dug up by badgers when trying to catch ground squirrels and other small mammals they feed on. Badgers walk low to the ground on short legs and are gray in appearance with white and brown visible in some places. Their tails are short and stubby. Faces have distinct black and white markings that are broken. These animals weigh between 12 and 20 pounds, with some individuals weighing more. Due to their short legs, badgers make furrows when walking in the snow.

I have heard reports of badgers claiming deer shot by hunters that fell near their dens. In at least one case, an animal had a deer almost completely underground before the hunter that shot the deer came along and found it.

Badgers inhabit fields, pastures, farmland, grasslands, and open terrain above timberline. They are found in all of the western and midwestern states and range northward into the plains and farmbelt of Canada.

A badger at its burrow entrance. (Photograph courtesy of Michigan Department of Natural Resources.)

Long front claws of badger are well suited for digging.

Skunks

There are two major species of skunks in North America—the striped and spotted. Their tracks are similar. Markings of the striped skunk are similar to those of the wolverine, except their bodies are black and the stripes along sides and markings on the head are white. Bushy, long-haired tails are similar in appearance between wolverines and skunks, too.

Skunks are walkers primarily, but when striped skunks run, they leave a track pattern characteristic of members of the weasel family—prints arranged in a diagonal line, one in front of the other. Running tracks of spotted skunks more often resemble those of a squirrel. When walking, feet are usually placed one ahead and slightly to the side of the other and leave impressions roughly

Badger track.

Striped skunk in a defensive position.

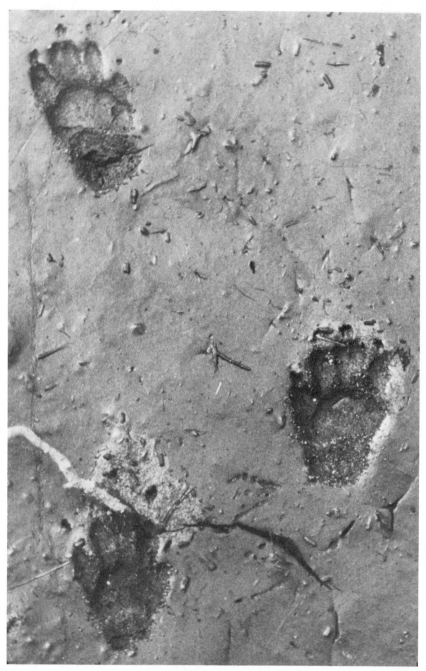

Striped skunk tracks in mud.

Spotted skunk. (Photograph courtesy of Leonard Lee Rue III.)

oval in shape. Short strides are characteristic of this animal. Five toes are present on each foot and claw marks are usually present in tracks, especially the longer ones of front feet. Tracks measure from 1¼ inches to almost 2 inches.

The skunk is well known for its defense mechanism, which is the ability to spray offensive-smelling liquid from its anal scent glands. Musk glands that produce strong, usually objectionable odors are what link members of the weasel family together. Few representatives of the weasel tribe are recognized for this other than the skunk, with the possible exception of the wolverine, which leaves scent in cabins and along traplines that they invade.

Color variations are common among striped skunks, with some individuals mostly to all black and others mostly white. Spotted skunks actually wear a number of broken white stripes, giving them a spotted appearance. Spotted skunks are smaller than the striped variety averaging between 1 and 3 pounds. Striped skunks weigh from 5 to 10 pounds.

Trail of a striped skunk with prints close together.

Striped skunks are distributed in each of the lower forty-eight states and well north in Canadian provinces, which is an indication they are found in a wide variety of habitats. Spotted skunks do not have a range quite as large, being absent from much of the midwest and northeast, including an area along the east coast south to Florida. They are also largely absent from Montana, North Dakota, and most of Canada.

Many skunks live in or near cities and towns, venturing forth at night to search for insects and food scraps discarded by people. Their tracks are commonly seen at or near garbage dumps. Dead skunks are a common sight along highways where they are killed by cars. One of the major predators of skunks are great horned owls, but other birds of prey and predatory mammals such as badgers also kill and eat them.

In connection with their search for larval insects or grubs, skunks dig shallow, cone-shaped holes in lawns, fields, and openings. Skunks also eat bird and turtle eggs and scavenge on road- or winter-killed animals. Broken egg shells littering a sandy area near a lake is a sure sign a skunk raided a nest of turtle eggs there.

4

Aquatic Mammals

THERE IS NO uniform track pattern among aquatic mammals such as beavers, otters, muskrats, and nutria. Furthermore, tracks may be the least obvious sign left by members of this group. The beaver is a perfect example.

Beavers

Last fall I was in several areas where beavers were abundant and looked carefully for their tracks, but found none. However, I did see several types of more obvious sign, one of which was tree-cutting activity. The animals were working on aspen or poplar trees situated near water in one particular area. Several trees had been felled, and the trunks of others were partially gnawed through.

Beavers fell trees by biting chunks of wood evenly all the way around the trunk, although some animals work only from one side. Chips of wood that are bitten out are dropped at the base of the trees. Partially gnawed trunks will often have an even band of wood removed all the way around. The animals continue chipping away until the gnawed trunk becomes too weak to support the tree and it topples over.

A beaver resting on the water. Note large, flat tail.

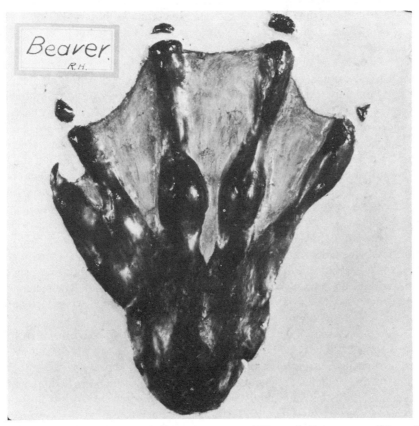

Hind footprint of a beaver. (Photograph courtesy of Wisconsin Department of Natural Resources.)

Once a tree is down, beavers often cut it into lengths, at least the limbs, that they can carry or drag into the water to feed on later. They eat the bark. In the fall, beavers in northern parts of the country store as much food as possible in a central location called "feed beds" for their use during the winter when ice covers their pond. Tips of freshly cut tree branches can sometimes be seen protruding above the water in beaver ponds, marking the location of feed beds. The animals may eat the bark from tree trunks themselves where they fall.

Wide paths marked by flattened vegetation and furrowed banks usually develop along routes beavers follow from the water to their cutting operation. These paths are sometimes referred to as beaver slides, and the animals may indeed slide into the water on them where they lead down steep banks. The print of a big webbed hind foot may appear in the mud or snow near slides, but not often. The reason beaver tracks are not frequently seen is that their big, flat tail dragging behind them erases the prints as they walk.

Sometimes beavers start to work on a tree and never finish, evident by dark, dried out wood where the tree was gnawed. I have seen a number of trees in this condition and can only guess why the job was never finished. Perhaps the animal was killed by a predator or trapped before the cutting could be completed. Or maybe the animal found a tree of a more desirable species to work on. There is also the possibility that beavers are absent-minded and may occasionally forget where they were working.

One summer in Quebec, Tom Huggler and I came across several trees a beaver felled, leaving stumps at least head high. At first glance, it might appear that beavers grow awfully big in that province, however, that was not the case. The trees were apparently gnawed down during winter or spring when there was still a lot of snow on the ground, accounting for the height of the cuts.

Howard and Nancy Stuckman, who operate a small general store along the Two Hearted River in Michigan's Upper Peninsula, have a white birch, beaver totem pole in their living room. The pole extends from the floor to the ceiling and is gnawed at regular intervals along its length. The pattern of gnawings was obviously in response to a steadily increasing accumulation of snow, which that region is noted for.

Light-colored chunks of wood varying in size on which the bark has been completely gnawed off are common along the banks of rivers and lakes frequented by beavers. These chewed pieces of wood are also used in the construction of dams, another prominent beaver sign. Dams are nothing more than walls of sticks and mud that slow the flow of water on streams and rivers, forming beaver ponds. These dams sometimes flood roads, causing damage in some cases. Dams on streams with fast water and heavy spring runoff are sometimes washed out, leaving remnants of the structure along

White birch beaver "totem pole" at upper Michigan residence.

A beaver dam. (Photograph courtesy of Michigan Department of Natural Resources.)

A beaver lodge.

banks. Old beaver ponds may eventually fill in and form meadows over a period of many years.

Beaver houses or lodges are large, dome-shaped structures that the animals live in. The outside is often covered with barkless pieces of wood and mud, like dams. These houses have an underwater entrance that leads into a chamber situated above the water's surface. Some beavers also live in holes or burrows along the banks of rivers.

Another sign beavers leave is scent posts that can usually be detected by smell as well as sight. The animals place a pile of mud and grass or other debris that can be as much as a foot in height, on the bank on which they secrete a sweet-smelling liquid from their castor glands located near the base of tails. The smell of this oil is so pleasing to humans (as it probably is to beavers) it is used in perfume.

I spotted a beaver on the bank of a stream from a Michigan highway on one occasion, and I stopped to try to photograph the animal. As I neared the location, the strong smell of castor was obvious. My nose led me to the scent post the animal was in the process of making when I saw it.

Beaver scats are deposited underwater. The animals are generally brown in color, but may be blonde or black. Their scaly, paddlelike tail is their most distinctive feature, which they use to slap the water when alarmed. The

A muskrat has a tail flattened from top to bottom.

Muskrat tracks from a display at the Seney National Wildlife Refuge, Michigan.

animals weigh between 20 and 50 or 60 pounds, on the average, but weights over 100 pounds have been recorded. These important furbearers are found throughout North America with the exception of most of Florida and areas along the east coast, parts of California, Arizona, Nevada, and north-central Texas.

Muskrats

Muskrat tracks are seen more often than those of beaver in mud near water. Their long hind feet are not noticeably webbed, and may measure about 3 inches long. Five toes are present. The smaller front feet show four distinct toes. A much smaller thumb on the inside usually is not visible in tracks. One of the most distinct features about the muskrat track is a wavy line between prints, which is a drag mark left by the tail.

Their tail is naked like other rats, but is not round. It has flat sides from top to bottom which propel the animals while swimming. Muskrats some-times leave water to head cross-country during the fall and winter, and their

A marsh filled with muskrat houses. (Photograph courtesy of Michigan Department of Natural Resources.)

A nutria. Notice round tail and outside toe of hind foot not webbed. (Photograph courtesy of Leonard Lee Rue III.)

tracks or the animals themselves, may show up some distance from water as a result.

Muskrat houses are generally obvious in marshes occupied by these animals. They are dome-shaped like those built by beavers, but are much smaller, usually less than four feet in height, and are constructed with aquatic vegetation. Houses or huts used by muskrats may be numerous and situated close to one another where the animals are abundant. These furbearers burrow into banks, too, like beavers. Holes leading into burrows are normally underwater and not visible unless water levels drop.

Muskrats feed mostly on vegetation, although, I once saw one eating a fish, and they also eat mussels. The animals dig in mud along banks for roots and bulbs, leaving signs of their activity. Stalks of bank-growing vegetation are also cut by muskrats. Mats of cut vegetation mark feeding beds in favored dining areas.

Scats are common in clusters on logs and rocks in the water, and other frequently used resting places. The droppings are elongated pellets and measure about a half-inch in length.

These animals are brown in color and much smaller than beavers, averaging between 2 and 4 pounds, a little less in some locations. Florida water rats are closely related to muskrats. They are smaller in size and have round, instead of flat, tails. They leave sign identical to muskrats, and are only found in the Okefenokee Swamp, shared by Georgia and Florida, where muskrats do not occur. The range of muskrats is similar to that of beavers, although they are not found as far north in Canada and Alaska, and they are largely absent from Texas.

Nutria

Nutria exhibit characteristics similar to both beavers and muskrats and, in fact, could pass as a hybrid between the two. Bodily, they look like beaver, but their tail is ratlike and round. The nutria's large hind feet are webbed, but webbing only includes four toes. The fifth toe on the outside of the foot is independent of the others. That characteristic alone should help differentiate between beaver and nutria tracks. Prints left by nutria are more commonly seen than those of beaver because they do not possess a large flat tail to erase them.

These furbearers construct feed beds similar to muskrats, only larger. Nutria normally weigh less than 20 pounds, but more than 15. They burrow into banks along bodies of water they occupy. Native to South America, nutria were introduced in the United States and are found in Louisiana, east Texas, Arkansas, southern Mississippi and into Florida. Populations have also been

A pair of otter on the ice with one about to pick up a fish it dropped.

Otter tracks from a display at the Seney National Wildlife Refuge, Michigan. Note that webbing does not show.

OTTER ($\frac{1}{2}$ size)

Continuous furrow in the snow left by an otter traveling overland.

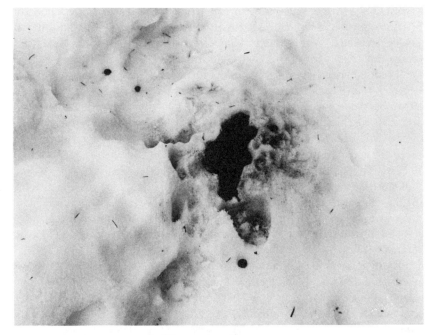

Otter scat on the snow.

established in scattered locations in states such as North Carolina, Virginia, Kentucky, Ohio, Idaho, Washington, and Oregon.

Otters

River otters are actually members of the weasel family, but since they spend much of their time in and around water, they deserve mention in this chapter. All four feet are webbed, although the front feet are more lightly webbed than the rear, with five toes on each foot. Webbing is not always visible in their tracks, especially front footprints.

I recently saw the tracks of a pair of otters in the snow that were traveling together cross-country. Both animals left continuous furrows in the snow with paired tracks at regular intervals. The webbing on hind feet was visible in many prints, but not in impressions left by front feet. I have seen similar tracks made by otters, usually single animals, during other winters as well. Webbing may not be visible in any tracks when otters tread on sand and ice.

Long, narrow bodies coupled with short legs are why otters generally plow their way through the snow. Hind legs are longer than front ones. Even in shallow snow, the animals seem to slide along as much as they bound. Look for otter tracks in mud along rivers, streams, lakes, and ponds during snowless seasons. Webs usually show in tracks made in mud. Hind feet average less than 3 inches in length with front feet smaller.

It is not unusual to see the tracks of two or three otters traveling together. The times I have seen otters in the fall they appeared to be in family groups. I also observed and photographed a pair together in the spring that were sunning themselves on the ice of a pool at the Seney National Wildlife Refuge in upper Michigan. When they got hungry, they entered the water through a hole in the ice and were only gone short periods of time before reappearing with fish. The animals appear to be excellent fishermen.

Otter scats are watery, not holding together well and the mass measures 3 to 5 inches across. Fish scales and bones, plus remains of crayfish may appear in their scats. Droppings I have noticed are black in color and may be found on logs, rocks, beaver dams, or in the snow when they travel overland.

These animals are generally brown in color, but may look black. They have long, fully-haired tails that are thick at the base and taper to a point at the end. Their primary range includes much of Canada and Alaska, plus northern states in the west, Great Lakes region, and northeast. Otters are also found in a block of states in the southeastern United States.

5

Rabbits and Hares

THE TRACK PATTERN of rabbits and hares is roughly triangular in shape, consisting of oval to oblong hind feet prints planted side by side, with the smaller, almost circular prints of front feet appearing behind them, usually one in front of the other. Major differences of tracks from one species to another is in size of imprints left by feet, but there are some other variations.

Rabbit or hare tracks most closely resemble those left by squirrels. However, there should not be much difficulty distinguishing between the two, if for no other reason than squirrel tracks go from tree to tree while rabbit tracks seldom lead to trees larger than saplings, unless they have fallen or their base is associated with ground cover where a rabbit might seek shelter. Beyond that, footprints left by squirrels show both front and back feet paired, whereas prints of front feet of rabbits are seldom paired. Where toes of the hind feet are visible in squirrel tracks, five are present. Four toes show in rabbit tracks when visible.

Rabbits

The two primary species of so-called rabbits in North America are cottontails and jackrabbits, with the snowshoe or varying hare the most common representative of that species, although there are Arctic hares in the far northern reaches of Canada and Alaska. Cottontails are actually the only true wild rabbit native to North America. The difference between rabbits and hares is that the young of rabbits are born naked with their eyes closed, whereas hares are furred when born and have their eyes open. The young of "jackrabbits" fall into the latter category.

Cottontails

Measurements of the length of the track pattern (from the base to the tip of the imaginary triangle) of cottontails vary from 7 to 12 inches in length. Tracks of hind feet themselves average about 3 inches in length, twice as

Cottontail curled up in a hollow log. (Photograph courtesy of Michigan Department of Natural Resources.)

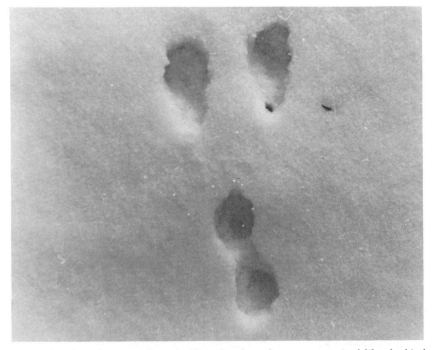

Triangular-shaped cottontail track. Note that front feet are not paired like the hind ones.

long as front footprints. There are at least eight relatives of the cottontail, some of which are subspecies; including eastern, mountain, New England, brush, desert, swamp, marsh and pygmy rabbits. They vary in weight from less than a pound to at least 3 pounds, obviously resulting in variations in track size.

Distance between normal cottontail hops is 10 to 14 inches. When hopping, hind feet are fairly uniform in width from front to back. However, the four toes on hind feet will usually be spread when running, increasing track width at the front. Rabbit tracks are not observed regularly until snow covers the ground, except in sandy or muddy areas the animals might hop across.

These rabbits have relatively short ears and are basically brown in color, except for their cottonball-like tails that are prominent as they run, although the tail is not white on several close relatives such as pygmy, marsh, swamp, and brush rabbits. Sign other than tracks to look for are droppings, feeding activity, and forms. Rabbit scats are circular, pill-shaped, and pill-sized pellets that are brown in color. It is difficult to mistake them for anything else.

When feeding, rabbits clip twigs neatly, leaving a clean-cut diagonal edge. They choose twigs close to the ground. Deer also feed on tips of brush, but they *break them off* rather than bite through the stem because deer do not have teeth on top in front, only on the bottom. Consequently, twigs deer feed on have rough, uneven edges. Cottontails also gnaw the bark from saplings and fallen trees, leaving the light-colored inner wood visible where they have fed. The snow or ground where they feed is normally covered with droppings. When snow is present, it is packed down where rabbits have stopped and eaten.

Cottontails typically seek shelter under brushpiles or in patches of brushy cover. This is where forms will be found, which are nothing more than nests or beds where rabbits rest and hide for the day, and are marked by shallow depressions. Rabbits have a tendency to circle back toward their forms when jumped from them and tracked or trailed by hounds. Cottontails are also at home in woodpiles, lumber piles, in burrows, and under buildings. That is why they are often seen in cities. Marsh and swamp rabbits, as their name implies, search out wetter, lower-lying habitat than their relatives.

Combined ranges of the eastern and mountain cottontails encompass most of the lower forty-eight states, with the exceptions of Maine, Vermont, New Hampshire, most of California, and the westernmost portions of Oregon and Washington. The mountain variety resides in the west, and the eastern in the midwest, south, and east with some overlap along a jagged line from northeast New Mexico to northwest North Dakota. The New England variety is estab-

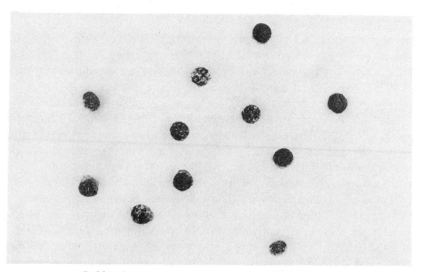

Rabbit droppings, which are similar for all species.

A twig nipped off by a hare. Rabbits cut twigs in the same manner.

A white-tailed jackrabbit at the entrance to its winter form. These forms can sometimes be spotted from long distances by dirty snow. (Photograph courtesy of F. R. Martin.)

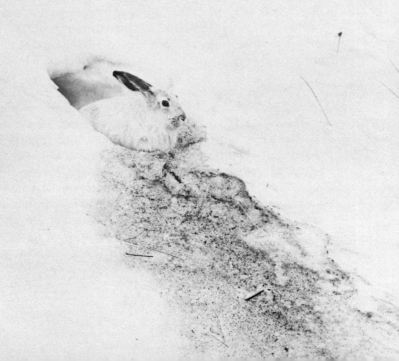

lished in Vermont, New Hampshire, Massachusetts, New Jersey, Rhode Island, Connecticut, eastern New York, most of Pennsylvania, and parts of the Virginias and Carolinas.

Desert cottontails are at home in the southwest, but are found northward through Colorado, Wyoming, and into Montana, and south into Mexico. The belt-shaped range of brush rabbits extends south along the coast from Oregon into Mexico. Pygmy rabbits dwell in northern Nevada, southwestern Idaho, eastern Oregon, and into small parts of Washington and California. Southeastern states of Arkansas, Mississippi, Alabama, Louisiana, and eastern Texas are the home of the swamp rabbit. Marsh rabbits have established themselves throughout Florida, and north along the coast into parts of Georgia and the Carolinas.

Jackrabbits

The two most common jackrabbits are white and black-tailed, with the blacktail being the smaller of the two. Hind foot tracks of blacktails measure about 2½ inches in length when hopping, as opposed to 3½ inches for whitetails. Only prints from the front portion of hind feet register while hopping, unlike cottontails and snowshoes. When the animals stop, heels are lowered and also leave imprints. So tracks made by hind feet of resting whitetail jacks will be longer, about 6 to 7 inches, than when hopping. Similar tracks of the blacktail will be slightly shorter.

Track patterns of blacktails are 9 to 12 inches deep, and hops of 10 inches are average. Whitetails have track patterns that measure about 17 inches, with distance between tracks ranging from 1 to 2 feet.

As their names suggest, these jackrabbits can be distinguished by the color of their tails. Blacktails also have longer ears than their cousins and do not change color in the winter. In the northern part of their range, whitetails turn white in the winter and their ears become black. Their legs are too long, their size too big, and their habitat too open to be mistaken for snowshoe hares.

Whitetails weigh from 6 to 8 pounds or more, and blacktails may weigh as much as 7 pounds, but are generally around 5 or 6 pounds, sometimes less. It would take an exceptionally large varying hare to weigh 6 pounds.

The larger variety of jackrabbit is found over a much greater area than the blacktail, residing in all of the western states and some in the midwest—the Dakotas, plus parts of Minnesota, Iowa, and Wisconsin. They do best on open plains. Blacktails occupy more arid regions and are commonly found in sagebrush. They are distributed throughout Kansas, plus portions of Oklahoma, Colorado, Utah, Idaho, Nevada, Oregon, and Washington.

Jackrabbit droppings are similar to those from cottontails, only a little

Black-tailed jackrabbits have longer ears than whitetails. (Photograph courtesy of Karl Maslowski.)

larger. Feeding sign is similar when they eat brush, although jacks feed on cactus plants in desert areas, too. Jackrabbit forms can be found under bushes, next to rocks, or in the open.

Whitetail jacks use the same form day after day during the winter and are continually forced to dig out after a snowfall. Snow tunnels develop as a result that are sometimes marked by dirt at the entrance. Jackrabbit forms can sometimes be spotted from a distance by looking for patches of dirty snow.

Hares

Snowshoe hare tracks are the most familiar to me among members of the rabbit family. Their big hind feet leave prints that average 6 inches in

Snowshoe hare in its winter coat.

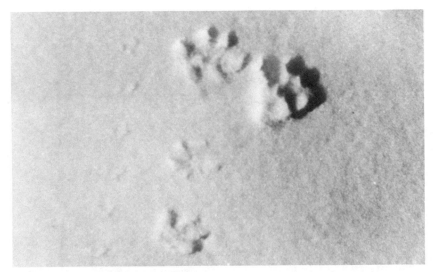

Track pattern of a snowshoe hare. Note four toes on hind feet.

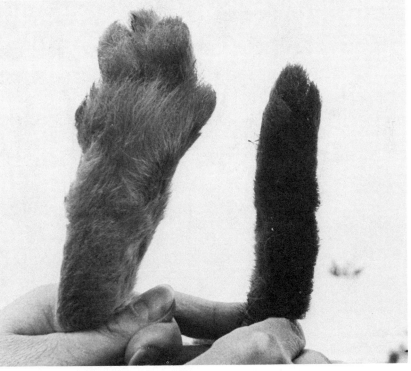

Comparison between hind feet of a snowshoe and a cottontail.

Rabbits or hares ate the bark from these saplings. Bark at the highest point on the trees was gnawed during the winter when deeper snow enabled them to reach higher than usual.

length. In deep snow the animals spread their toes to better support their weight, leaving tracks that are wide at the front and taper down toward the heel. The snowshoe's track pattern is 10 to 11 inches in length, and normal hops cover 10 to 14 inches.

These hares most often weigh between 3 and 4 pounds. They are brown during the summer and gradually turn white, except for black-tipped ears, from fall to winter. However, there is a hare in Washington state, related to the snowshoe, that remains brown year round. Ear length on snowshoes is intermediate between that of cottontails and jackrabbits. They inhabit lowland swamps and evergreen thickets during the winter, but can be found in upland habitat at other times of the year.

Their range includes northernmost states in the lower forty-eight, but extends south in the west in correspondence with mountain ranges and evergreen forests, and as far south as Tennessee in the east. Most of Canada and Alaska and their abundant northern forest are also home to these hares.

Scats and feeding sign of the snowshoe are very much like those of cottontails, eating bark of saplings and fallen trees, especially aspen, and twigs. However, droppings are slightly larger. Forms are located under the protective boughs of evergreen trees, in brushpiles and stumps and other dense cover. The animals will burrow into the snow for protection from the elements during inclement weather, although they spend far less time in such hideouts than cottontails. Where both cottontails and snowshoes occur together, the size of their tracks usually differentiates between the two.

Varying hares pack down trails over routes they travel regularly. Outdoor people who find themselves in a rough survival situation in northern forests where snowshoes occur can catch hares by setting a snare with a shoelace, fishing line, or piece of wire on such a trail. Urine from snowshoes often stains the snow orange and is sometimes mistaken for blood.

These hares are as apt to circle when trailed as cottontails, perhaps even more so. I have spent many days tracking them and it is not unusual to have them follow the same circle time and time again. Hunters or photographers who are familiar with this tactic can often get a look at the animals by cutting across the circle or starting after a hare, then quickly backtracking to the starting point to wait for the rabbit's return.

Hare populations, including jackrabbits, are subject to extreme highs and lows that sometimes occur on regular cycles of so many years. The reasons for these population cycles are not fully understood. The animals become so abundant at times they all but eliminate their food supply, then disease and parasites take over and dramatically reduce populations. Such dramatic highs and lows are less common where the animals are routinely hunted, which is not only better for the hares themselves, but their habitat as well.

6

Small Mammals

THE SMALLEST MAMMALS—shrews, mice and voles—leave tracks of a size that cannot be mistaken for anything else. Miniature track patterns are obviously the work of one small mammal or another. When hopping, these small mammals make track patterns like those of tree squirrels with paired imprints from front and rear feet. Impressions of hind feet appear in front of those of forefeet in sand, mud, or little snow. Only two depressions from feet are usually visible in soft snow an inch or more in depth. Drag marks from tails may or may not show, depending upon the animal that left the prints.

White-footed deer mice leave a distinctive track pattern in which drag marks from their long tails always show, sometimes with a distinct break in the line from track to track, and at other times almost continuous. Shorter tailed meadow voles leave short drag marks to the rear of track patterns when hopping in soft snow. No evidence of the tail may show in sand, mud, or a skiff of snow. The same is true when meadow voles walk.

Shrews such as the short-tailed variety, as well as other species, drag their tails in the snow when walking or running. However, track patterns of shrews are generally smaller and narrower than those of deer mice. Shrew

A masked shrew. Note pointed snout and small eyes. (Photograph courtesy of Leonard Lee Rue III.)

A deer mouse. (Photograph courtesy of Leonard Lee Rue III.)

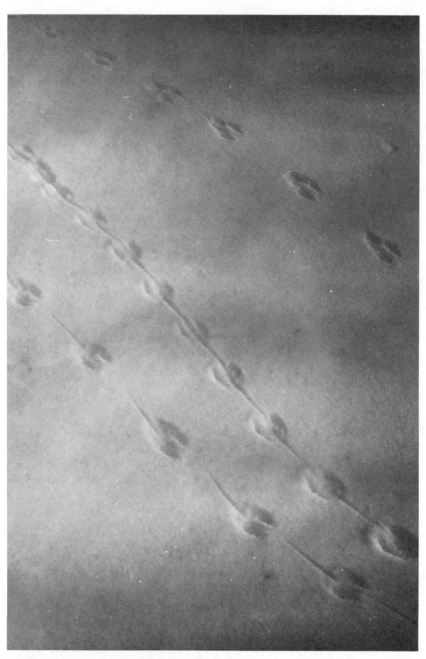

Tracks of deer mice. (Photograph courtesy of Michigan Department of Natural Resources.)

A hamsterlike meadow vole.

trails may measure an inch in width, sometimes a little more. Track patterns made by deer mice are between 1½ and 2 inches wide.

Small mammals spend most of their time under grass or forest litter such as leaves, where they have networks of paths or tunnels. Few days go by when sitting in woods with the ground carpeted in leaves during the fall without hearing shrews, mice, and voles scurrying about underneath leaves, and they sometimes show themselves briefly when venturing into the open. The high-pitched squeaks they make are clues to their presence, in addition to the noise they make rustling leaves.

These animals also form tunnels under the snow, sometimes pushing up walls of snow around them when snow depths are minimal, or a fresh blanket of soft snow falls on top of a layer of crusted snow. The walls of snow around mouse or shrew tunnels are so thin they break apart in some places.

Nests of mice, voles, and shrews may be found in grassy fields, under logs and brush, in bushes or underground, plus any sheltered location in woodland cabins that are either abandoned or only temporarily occupied. Mice and voles eat seeds, vegetable matter, and insects primarily, with shrews being more meat eaters, concentrating on insects. They sometimes even kill and eat mice.

Deer mice are brown to gray in color with white undersides, fairly long tails, large eyes and ears. Other mice are similar in appearance, but may or may not have white undersides. Voles are also gray and brown in color, but

Vole tracks, both walking and hopping. Note short drag mark from tail in hopping prints.

A star-nosed mole with shovellike front feet and snout encircled with fleshy appendages.

are chunkier like hampsters and have short tails. Their ears and eyes are much smaller than those of mice, too. Shrews have pointed snouts as opposed to the more rounded faces of mice and snub-nosed appearance of voles. Shrews are usually gray or brown in color, but may look black, with tails usually shorter than mice. Their eyes and ears are very small, with the ears almost impossible to see.

Mice and shrews of one species or another are found throughout North America. Deer mice have the widest distribution, found practically everywhere except some states in the southeast. Meadow voles range as far north as Alaska, over most of Canada and the northern two-thirds of the lower United States, with the exception of far western states. The range of masked shrews is similar to meadow voles. Shorttail shrews are found over the entire eastern half of the lower United States and into Canada.

Moles

Tracks of moles are not a reliable sign because they seldom venture above ground. However, one type of sign these animals do make that can be seen is raised ridges of soil at ground level, which can be 3 inches or more in height and 6 inches in diameter, that serve as walls for tunnels just under the surface. These differ from similar sign left by gophers that consist of ropes of soil, which are solid underneath. They are made of dirt that line the sides of gopher tunnels under the snow and form solid soil casts when the snow melts.

Moles also push irregular mounds of dirt (molehills) above ground that may or may not be connected to ridges of soil that mark tunnels. These can usually be distinguished from mounds of dirt marking the entrance of gopher burrows because there will be no evidence of an entrance along an edge of the mound. Entrances to gopher holes are often plugged with dirt, but the outlines of them are visible nonetheless.

There are a number of species of moles, with the eastern and starnose being the most widespread. They are gray, black, and brown in color with pointed snouts like shrews and have short tails. Eyes are sometimes covered with skin, and ears are not apparent. Their front feet are large and paddlelike with long claws for digging. Front feet are also off to the sides of the body with palms turned upward in most cases.

The starnose is the mole I am most familiar with. They have a distinct, fleshy appendage on the ends of their noses with twenty-two short, fingerlike tentacles that resemble a star. The animals have noticeably fat tails that increase in diameter between the base and tip. Starnose moles remain active during the winter and are good swimmers, sometimes entering ponds, lakes, or streams.

These moles are apparently not favored items in the diets of typical predators, because I have encountered several that were killed and not eaten while trailing both bobcats and coyotes. The last starnose I found was on the edge of a freshly plowed woods road during the winter. There were several inches of snow covering the road before it was plowed. Apparently the mole was burrowing its way under the snow in the road when the plow came along, killing it.

Moles eat worms and insect larvae, plus some vegetable matter. Eastern moles are distributed across the eastern half of the United States, except a band of northernmost states. The starnose inhabits the northeastern United States and Canada, plus the Great Lakes region. Townsend, California, and Pacific moles are found along the west coast.

Pikas

The small, rabbitlike pika seldom leaves tracks because it lives in rocks of mountainous regions in the western United States and Canada into Alaska. Pikas resemble miniature cottontails without the tail, and can be gray and brown in color. Their scats are small pellets resembling those of rabbits, and they accumulate "haystacks" consisting of dried grass and vegetation in the rocks where they live as food for the winter.

Raised ridge of ground crossing woods road marks underground tunnel of eastern mole.

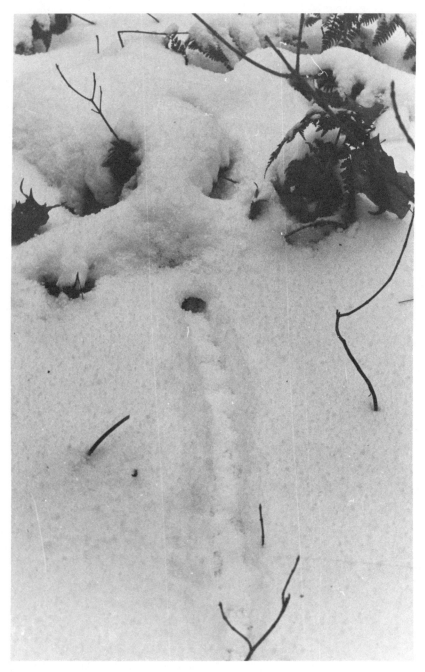

Small mammal trail in soft snow emerges from a pile of snow-covered vegetation.

A pika carries a mouthful of vegetation to add to its haystack.

Rats

Wood or packrats are one of the most common type of rat found in the wild, concentrated primarily in western North America, including Canada, states in the lower United States, and into Mexico. Their larger-than-mouse, smaller-than-squirrel tracks are sometimes seen in the sand. They have large, oval-shaped pads on the tips of toes, with five toes on hind feet and four on front. Track patterns of woodrats most closely resemble those of rabbits, but are smaller. Woodrats are brown or gray in color with long, round tails that taper to a point.

These animals are nest builders and commonly use sticks and twigs as building materials. However, anything can show up in a packrat nest including bottle caps, pull tabs from cans, cans themselves, bones, and anything else the animals find suitable. Nests are often in cactus, rocks, bushes, old shacks, and even in trees. Woodrat scats are slender pellets and are usually present near nests, sometimes accumulating into large black masses in the rocks. Urine deposits stain rocks white or yellow under woodrat and pika burrows.

Norway rats commonly live in cities throughout North America wherever they can find a place to hide. They may reside in burrows in the ground, usually coming out at night to feed on food items discarded by people. Norway rats are also at home at garbage dumps where they live in piles of discarded debris or burrows. Scats of Norway rats are slender pellets.

Common Norway rat. (Photograph courtesy of Leonard Lee Rue III.)

Kangaroo rats are residents of the desert where their tracks can sometimes be seen in the sand. When hopping, they leave two prints less than an inch long side by side like those of weasels in the snow. Their front feet do not touch the ground when traveling in this manner and they hop on their toes, so only the front portion of hind feet leave tracks, much the same as jackrabbits. When moving slowly or feeding, small, circular prints of front feet will appear between impressions of hind feet that will average 1½ inches in length with the heel showing. Drag marks from their long, brush-tipped tails are often visible in conjunction with this track pattern.

The nests of kangaroo rats consist of mounds of sand as much as 3 feet high with a number of holes in them. Some of the entrances may be plugged with sand. Trails used by these animals radiate from nests. Shallow depressions in the sand may also be visible nearby where they dust themselves.

Kangaroo rats have a unique appearance with huge hind feet out of proportion to the rest of their bodies. They hop upright on those feet like kangaroos. Their tails are long and have bushy tips. They are various shades of brown, with white low on their sides.

BUSINESS REPLY MAIL
FIRST-CLASS MAIL   PERMIT NO. 22   TAMPA FL

POSTAGE WILL BE PAID BY ADDRESSEE

**FIELD &
STREAM** ®

OUTDOOR LIFE ®
THE SPORTSMAN'S AUTHORITY SINCE 1898

PO BOX 61379
TAMPA   FL   33661-1379

7

Cats

CAT TRACKS, WHETHER made by the domestic variety or one of the three species of wild cats in North America—bobcat, lynx, and mountain lion—are basically circular in shape, exhibit four toes and do not, as a rule, leave marks from toenails in their prints. This is because cats walk with their claws sheathed, having the ability to extend them when needed for climbing or catching prey.

Clearly defined prints left by a member of the cat family are not likely to be mistaken for those of other species of wildlife. However, confusion may arise in situations where powdery snow or soft sand fails to register a distinct imprint of feet. Under these circumstances, it can be difficult at times to distinguish between bobcat and coyote or fox tracks. Spoor left by these animals are similar in size.

In situations where there is a question about whether a canine or feline made a track, look closely at the front edge of prints for any sign of marks left by toenails. The nails in the middle of the foot are often most pronounced in coyote and fox tracks. If deep snow is involved, toenails may leave narrow grooves in front of toes as they sink in the snow. Evidence of toenails is enough proof that a fox, coyote, or other animal of similar size with non-retractable nails planted a foot on the spot, not a cat.

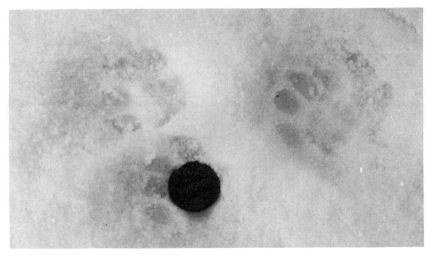

House cat tracks, a little larger than a penny.

Follow the tracks for a short distance frontwards, backwards, or both to look for a more distinct print if the ones encountered initially are impossible to distinguish. Under sandy conditions the animal may step in a spot where the soil is more compact and conducive to recording an accurate imprint of the bottom of the animal's foot. In the snow, check tracks where the animal walked under an evergreen tree or heavy brush where snow will be shallower than in the open.

There are other clues to look for, too, if a clear view of the tracks themselves is impossible. Bobcats, for example, regularly walk up on and along logs or fallen tree trunks and even on the rails of railroad tracks. I once followed a bobcat that walked on a rail for at least a quarter mile. Coyotes and foxes cross logs and fallen trees, but seldom walk on them for any distance.

And if any scat is present, check to see if the animal attempted to cover it. Members of the cat clan customarily try to cover their droppings with front feet, leaving scratch marks in the soil or snow around the scat, unless the soil is too hard. Coyotes and foxes do not attempt to cover their scat, although they sometimes rake the ground with their hind feet after defecating. Scratch marks left by wild canines are usually off to one side of the scat.

Cats generally place one foot in front of the other when walking in snow, leaving a neat row of tracks. Hind feet are slightly smaller than the front ones. When running, footprints are bunched together or in a staggered line with at least 2½ feet separating impressions. Members of the cat family are not as prone to trot or run when traveling or chased as wild canines are. If

Cat scat.

A bobcat with black on top of tail tip and white underneath. (Photograph courtesy of Michigan Department of Natural Resources.)

increased speed is called for cats simply walk fast whenever possible. How-ever, this is not necessarily true when it comes to securing prey.

Tracks left by domestic cats measure from 1 to 1½ inches in length and width, with from 5 to 8 inches between tracks. When running, house cats leave tracks about 2½ feet apart, sometimes a little more. House cat tracks are most often seen in residential areas or near farms in rural settings. How-ever, feral cats are found in some areas and their tracks may show up miles from human habitations. Populations of feral cats sometimes become estab-lished at garbage dumps.

Bobcats

Bobcat tracks range from 1¾ to 3½ inches in width and 1¾ to 2½ inches long. Width measurements of tracks from one animal can vary con-siderably depending upon the type of material they are imprinted in. When walking in deep snow, for example, cats spread their toes for support, leaving

Bobcat track. Notice no toenail marks are present.

tracks wider than normal. Distance between bobcat tracks while walking range from 9 to 14 inches. A distance of 3 to 3½ feet separates running tracks.

A trait of bobcats to keep in mind during the winter is they sometimes cross roads in the same place time after time. If deep snow is present, an animal may step in exactly the same depressions left during the previous crossing.

Bobcats are generally solitary animals, but the tracks of a female with her kittens may be seen into the fall. I have also encountered the tracks of mated pairs traveling together during late winter and into spring. The larger prints are usually those of the male. Bobcats range between 15 and 30 pounds in weight, but weights of 60 pounds or more have been recorded. The animals breed from February through April.

They have the widest distribution of any of the North American wild cats. Their range includes most of the United States. The largest vacancy in their range is in the lower midwest where there are few, if any, in Ohio, Indiana, Illinois, Iowa, the northern two-thirds of Missouri, eastern South Dakota, plus the southern portions of Minnesota, Wisconsin, and Michigan. Portions of Kentucky, North Carolina, Virginia, Maryland, Pennsylvania, New Jersey, Massachusetts, and New York are void of bobcats, too, in addition to all of Connecticut and Delaware. In Canada, the bobcat is established in southern portions of British Columbia, Alberta, Saskatchewan, Manitoba, Ontario, Quebec, and all of New Brunswick.

In the east and midwest, bobcats commonly inhabit lowland swamps with thick cover, but they can also be found in hilly country with rock caves. Rugged terrain that is rocky and mountainous, or that has thick brush is favored in the west, although these bob-tailed cats frequent the arid southwest where none of these conditions exist. Bobcats frequently travel along the course of rivers and creeks and may walk river ice in the winter to escape deep snow on the banks. Heavy cover surrounding some lakes is attractive to bobcats, too.

Bobcats vary widely in color from one part of their range to another, but their bobbed tail is a good identifying feature. The tail has a black spot on top near the end, but is white at the tip. A tuft of black hair sticks up from the tip of each ear. Growths of hair called ruffs grow out of the sides of the head and extend downward below the chin.

Due to the bobcat's habit of covering its scat, this type of sign is not seen often, except in parts of the west where the ground is too hard to permit the practice. Droppings that are not covered are normally 4 to 5 inches long and can be confused with those from coyotes, although constrictions in several places along its length are characteristic of bobcat dung. Scats may be broken into segments due to these constrictions. Some bobcats have favored locations for depositing waste.

Fairly straight trail of a bobcat.

Lynx

Lynx tracks are noticeably larger than those of the bobcat even though the animals average weights are similar (20 to 30 pounds for lynx). This is due to extra padding on the lynx's feet in the form of hair to increase their surface area for walking on snow like snowshoes. Prints left by lynx can even be as large as, and sometimes larger than, those of mountain lions. In snow, lynx sink less than mountain lions, and the width of their trail is generally narrower. Lynx leave a trail 6 to 8 inches wide, with a width of 8 to 13 inches typical for lions. Mountain lions sometimes leave a drag mark from their tails in deep snow, too, whereas this is impossible for lynx since their tails are shorter than those of bobcats.

Measurements of lynx tracks are 3 to 4½ inches in width and 4 to as much as 7 inches long in deep snow. Strides are from 7 to 14 inches when walking and about the same as a bobcat when running. Lynx sometimes take shorter steps than bobcat when walking in deep snow.

Lynx range throughout most of Canada and Alaska, and a few find their way into northern Minnesota, Michigan, New Hampshire, Vermont, and Maine. The principal range of this cat in the lower forty-eight is in mountainous regions of the west including parts of Colorado, Utah, Wyoming, Idaho, Montana, Washington, and Oregon. Since the lynx's primary prey is the snowshoe hare, it spends much of its time in thick, lowland habitat and mountain thickets that hares also frequent.

Ear tufts and ruffs are longer and more pronounced on lynx than bobcat, and the tip of the tail is black. Lynx appear larger than bobcats due to longer legs and hair, even though they may weigh the same. These animals breed during late winter into spring like bobcats.

Mountain Lions

Mountain lion tracks are 3 to 4½ inches wide and as much as 4 inches long, with a stride of 12 to 22 inches. Lions are capable of bounds of at least 5 feet when running.

Residents of the western United States and Canada have a better opportunity of seeing lion tracks than those living in the eastern half of either country, although there are a few locations in the east where mountain lions still live such as Arkansas, Florida, and New Brunswick in Canada. The animals have also been seen in Mississippi, Louisiana, Tennessee, the Carolinas, the Virginias, Vermont, Maine, Massachusetts, and New Hampshire. Unverified reports of lions have come from other states as well.

Mountain lions are most common in the following states: Washington, Oregon, Idaho, Nevada, Utah, Arizona, Wyoming, the western halves of

Tail tip of lynx are all black. They also have longer ear tufts than bobcats. (Photograph courtesy of Leonard Lee Rue III.)

Lynx tracks. (Photograph courtesy of National Park Service.)

Mountain lions are the largest member of the cat family in North America.

Montana and New Mexico, southern Texas, and much of California. In Canada, they roam through much of British Columbia and Alberta, plus parts of Manitoba and Saskatchewan. The large cats are also well established in Mexico.

Like its short-tailed relatives, mountain lions inhabit rugged, rocky, brushy country where its prey is most abundant. Large animals such as deer are the lion's favorite prey, although they do feed on smaller mammals, too. When a large animal is killed, lions commonly cover portions of the carcass they do not eat with leaves, twigs, grass, and other debris.

Mountain lions can be easily distinguished from other wild cats by their long tail and large size. Their overall length is from 7 to 8 feet, including 2½ to 3 feet of tail. And they range in weight from 100 to 175 pounds, with males over 200 pounds on record. Like the other cats, females are smaller than males. There is no distinct breeding season among mountain lions like the short-tailed cats.

Scats of mountain lions are similar to those left by bobcats, only larger in diameter, and are often buried. Droppings average about 5 inches in length with constrictions at various points along the length, or they may be in smaller segments.

Lions frequently scrape up mounds of soil to create scent posts they urinate on. Scratch marks are usually visible near these mounds and indicate which way the lion was traveling. As a rule, the animal continues in the direction it was facing when making the scent post. Dirt will be pulled backward when scratching.

Another sign characteristic of mountain lions is claw marks on tree trunks. Lions rake their claws along the bark to sharpen them. Bobcats and lynx do the same thing, but claw marks they leave are not as obvious as those left by mountain lions. Scratch marks left on trees by lions are not as deep as those made by black bears.

8

Canines

TRACKS MADE BY members of the dog family are characteristically oval or oblong in shape with toenails usually visible in prints. Front feet are larger than back feet. Anyone who owns a dog is probably familiar with the pattern. Clear prints show a large heel pad with four smaller toe pads in front of it. The two middle toes are situated side by side, with the outside ones opposite one another and further back. Nails on middle toes register in tracks most often.

Toe pads are arranged in a different pattern than those on the feet of cats. Cat toes are arranged in a neat, semi-circular row in front of heel pads. This characteristic can help distinguish between canine and feline tracks. For more information on differentiating between cat and dog tracks refer to the chapter on cats.

There is a way to determine the approximate weight of a dog, coyote, fox, or wolf using measurements of a track from a front foot. Multiply the width times the length then multiply the resultant figure by 5.

I tried this on my dog, which is a big hound, and the results were close. A front foot measured 4 × 3½ inches. The calculations produced a weight of 70 pounds. Charlie tipped the scales at 80 pounds the last time I weighed him.

Red fox with white-tipped tail.

Red fox track.

Wild members of the dog family include four species of foxes (red, gray, kit, and arctic), plus coyotes and wolves. In rural settings where free roaming domestic dogs are found, it is sometimes difficult to tell the difference between tracks left by pets and their wild relatives, although the size of prints can be helpful. Large farm dogs such as collies, shepherds, and mongrels have larger feet than coyotes or foxes. Where tracks of dogs are similar in size to those of wolves, coyotes, or foxes, behavior of the individual animals can help differentiate between them.

Dogs frequently walk along rural roads, for example, urinating on trees or brush at regular intervals, and may walk or run off the road for a short distance, then quickly return. This sign is most obvious when snow is covering the ground, of course. Coyotes, foxes and wolves, on the other hand, seldom spend much time on roads that receive much traffic. They either cross directly from one side to the other, sometimes on the run, or walk a short distance down the road before crossing. Occasionally, they will leave a road on the same side they entered.

This trait applies to roads that receive regular vehicular traffic where homes are located that domestic dogs would come from. Coyotes, foxes, and wolves regularly follow lightly used roads and trails that penetrate their home territory. Dogs are not normally seen along these thoroughfares, except possibly during hunting seasons when hunting dogs would be accompanied by their masters.

Foxes

Red Foxes

Red fox tracks are 2 to 2½ inches long, depending on whether front or back foot is measured. Distance between tracks when walking to trotting ranges from about 12 to 18 inches. The trail they leave in the snow is generally no wider than 4 inches. Reds are known for leaving tracks in a straight line, but this is not always true. Pads may not leave distinct impressions, if any at all, in the snow due to covering hair. As you can see in the photo by Jeff Bunker, the feet of red foxes are completely covered with hair during the winter. A unique feature of heel pads of red foxes (where clear prints are visible) is a raised bar across the pad that is roughly shaped like an inverted V.

Neither coyote nor gray fox feet have this feature. Coyote tracks are generally larger than those of red fox and those of gray fox are smaller. Marks from toenails are also more pronounced in coyote and especially gray fox tracks than those of red fox, during the winter at least, due to the amount of

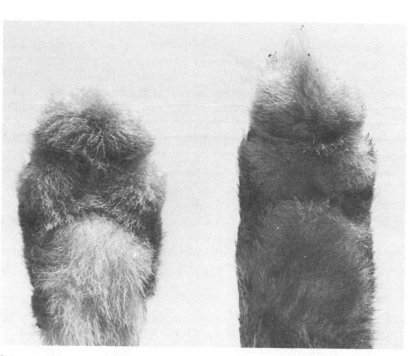

Hair-covered bottoms of feet of a red fox. The larger front foot is on the left. (Photograph courtesy of Jeff Bunker.)

Red fox scat on a rock. Raccoons will also defecate on rocks and logs. (Photograph courtesy of Scot Stewart.)

Red fox pup at den entrance. (Photograph courtesy of Michigan Department of Natural Resources.)

Gray fox with black on top of the tail and at the tip. (Photograph courtesy of Karl Maslowski.)

hair that grows on the bottom of red's feet then. In addition, coyotes sink further in the snow than lighter red foxes.

Red foxes mate during January, and the tracks of a male and female traveling together are common then.

This species of fox has a wider distribution than any of the other foxes, making itself at home in most of North America, including Alaska. However, there are a few areas where they are generally not found including most of Arizona and Montana, parts of California, New Mexico, Texas, Colorado, Oklahoma, Kansas, Nebraska, Wyoming, South Dakota, and Florida.

These foxes are often associated with agricultural areas where there is a mixture of fields and woodlands, but they are adaptable enough to survive in country that tends toward either extreme. They generally inhabit denser cover in the winter than other times of the year.

Even though this animal's coat is usually red in color, it can vary from yellowish to orange, and may be partially gray or even black on occasion with silver-tipped hairs. What are referred to as silver foxes are simply color mutations of the red. All "red" foxes have a white-tipped tail regardless of what color their coat actually is. Their feet and lower legs are black. Reds vary in weight from 7½ to 13 pounds, with females being smaller than males.

No effort is made to cover droppings, which may be seen along two-

Print of left front foot of a gray fox. (Photograph courtesy of Wisconsin Department of Natural Resources.)

Kit fox of the Southwest. (Photograph courtesy of Kent and Donna Dannen.)

A coyote or brush wolf.

track roads or wooded trails red foxes often travel. An accumulation of scats may be deposited one on top of the other. Scats are generally from 2 to 3 inches long and pointed at the ends. They are usually smaller in diameter (about a half-inch) than coyote droppings.

Red fox dens are another sign to look for. They are usually located in the open with more dirt around the opening than woodchuck dens. Tracks may be visible in excavated soil. Fur, feathers and bones from prey may be seen near the den, too.

Gray Foxes

Tracks of gray foxes are a little more than an inch to 1½ inches long. This animal's stride is generally 10 to 12 inches. Unlike other foxes, grays sometimes climb trees, where their long toenails come in handy. Pairs of grays travel together on a regular basis. Mating takes place in the winter.

Gray foxes range over much of the United States and into Mexico. They are largely absent from an area in the northcentral to northwest United States that extends as far south as Kansas. These foxes are more at home in thick brush and other cover than reds.

Grays have red coloration on their face and ears, but are largely gray in color. A black streak runs along the top of the tail, including the tip. Average weights of gray foxes range from 5 or 6 to 11 pounds.

Scats are deposited along wooded trails much the same as with red fox. Droppings from grays are usually smaller than those from reds with tapered ends. Gray fox dens are normally well hidden.

Kit Foxes

Swift and kit foxes leave prints a little over an inch to 1¾ inches in length and can be confused with those of gray fox where their ranges overlap. When walking, they place their feet 8 to 10 inches apart. Kit foxes are the

Coyote track. Notice how much more pronounced pads are than from red fox track. Coyotes do not grow as much hair on their feet as red foxes do. Toenail marks are also visible in this coyote track.

Front and rear feet of a coyote for comparison.

least common species, being found only in the southwestern United States and northern Mexico in dry, desert-type habitat. The kit and swift foxes are actually separate species, although the names are sometimes used interchangeably. They are similar in appearance with one variety having longer ears than the other. These small foxes are light in color and have black-tipped tails. Droppings are very similar to those of the gray fox.

Arctic Foxes

Tracks of the arctic fox overlap those of the red in size, but average larger, with lengths up to 2¾ inches. However, the animals themselves are seen as readily as their tracks, unlike other species of foxes. These animals are curious and not generally afraid of man. Their range is in the northern reaches of Canada and Alaska on the tundra.

Arctic foxes have a white or blue coat in the winter that changes to a brownish color for summer months. Their dens are marked by soil spread about the entrance. These animals weigh from 8 to 12 pounds.

Running track pattern of a coyote, which is similar for foxes and wolves.

Coyote scat with lots of hair in evidence.

Coyotes

Coyotes or brush wolves leave prints that measure from 2 to 2¾ inches long, with walking strides ranging from 13 to 15 inches apart. When running, tracks may be separated by 3 to as much as 8 or 10 feet, depending on snow depth or the lack of it. Trails left by walking coyotes in the snow are generally 4 to 6 inches in width. Brush wolves do not grow as much hair on the bottoms of their feet as red foxes do, so their pads normally show in tracks.

Like the red fox, coyotes mate in the winter (January and February), although that is not the only time the animals travel together. The tracks of family groups or packs containing a number of individuals are sometimes encountered.

Coyotes enjoy a wide distribution, ranging south into Mexico and as far north as Alaska. The southeastern United States and northeastern portions of Canada are the only locations where these animals are not firmly established.

Timber wolf.

Timber wolf tracks are large like this one.

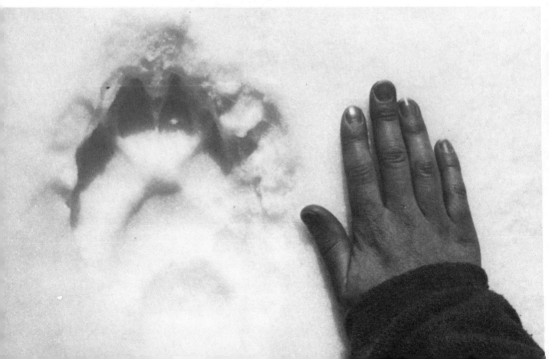

Prints of a pair of wolves traveling together. (Photograph courtesy of Jim Hammill.)

As might be guessed, coyotes are adaptable, occupying a variety of habitats from remote woodlands to the suburbs of large cities.

Color variations are common among coyotes like other wild dogs, although they generally appear gray in color, with a bushy tail tipped in black. Coyotes are much larger than gray foxes, weighing from 20 to 40 pounds. They carry their tails down when running as opposed to wolves, which carry theirs straight out or at an upward angle.

Coyote droppings are deposited in locations similar to those used by foxes. In fact, coyote and fox scats may be found on top of each other where their ranges overlap. Scats measure about 3 inches in length and up to an inch in diameter. Dens are well hidden like those of the gray fox.

Wolves

Timber or gray wolves have the largest tracks among wild canines, measuring from 4 to more than 5 inches in length. Alaskan wolves are larger than their relatives in Canada and the northern United States, leaving correspondingly larger tracks. Family groups and packs are common among wolves, so tracks of a number of wolves may be seen together. In the winter, packs often walk in single file leaving a well defined trail. Mating takes place in February. As a rule, only dominant members of a pack breed, not all adults as is the case among coyotes and foxes.

Canada and Alaska are the timber wolves' primary ranges, but they also roam in northern Minnesota, Wisconsin, Michigan, and Montana. Their habitat consists of barren tundra and expansive woodlands where rivers and lakes abound. Some wolves look like coyotes, only they are larger with weights ranging from 60 to well over 100 pounds. Some wolves are black and others are white.

Scats measure from 3 to 6 inches in length and an inch in diameter. Dens have large entrances and may have remains of prey nearby.

9

Bears

BEAR TRACKS ARE distinctive in their size and shape. Prints of front foot pads are wider than they are deep, and hind foot pads are longer than they are wide, resembling human feet somewhat, although tracks of the hind feet of bears taper off much more sharply toward the heel than human feet, and bears walk flat-footed without an arch. Imprints of five toes generally appear in front of foot pads. On front feet, a small heel pad is separate from the main pad and seldom shows in tracks unless they are made in soft mud or sand.

There are three species of bears in North America—black, grizzly, and polar—although grizzly and brown bears are sometimes thought to be different species by hunters. Brown bears are actually a large subspecies of the grizzly.

Black Bears

The front feet of average size black bears measure 3½ to 3¾ inches across, with hind feet averaging 6 to 7 inches in length including the toes. Young bears will have smaller tracks and older, heavier animals will generally leave larger prints. I measured the foot pads of a black bear that had a dressed weight of 520 pounds and found a front pad to be 6 inches across and a rear

Most black bears are black in color with brown snouts, like this one.

Black bear tracks, with print of hind foot in front of track from front foot. Notice that claw marks are not noticeable in prints.

pad 8½ inches long, not including the toes. The entire foot would have been at least 9 inches long.

Another black bear with a dressed weight estimated between 430 and 450 pounds had front foot pads that measured 4½ inches across. Rear pads were 5½ to 5¾ inches in length.

The tracks of a sow with one to three cubs can be seen from spring into fall. Black bears usually breed from late May into July, depending on location. The tracks of a boar and sow may be seen together during that period. Boars average larger than sows, as a rule.

Black bear tracks are usually smaller than those of grizzlies. However, the presence of claw marks in tracks and their location are also clues. The short claws of black bears do not often register in front of toes, except in very soft mud or sand, and when the animals are running. When claw marks appear in black bear tracks, they are usually directly in front of toes. The long, curved claws of grizzly and brown bears often show in tracks with a noticeable space between toe and claw prints.

Despite their name, some black bears are also various shades of brown, more so in western states, and other color phases including blue and white are present in Canada and Alaska. Brown black bears can be distinguished from grizzlies by the straight line profile of their backs. Grizzly and brown bears have a noticeable hump on their shoulders that black bear lack.

In weight, adult black bears average between 150 and 300 pounds, lighter than many people realize. Blacks that weigh upwards of 500 to 600 pounds are not unusual, but they are by no means common either. So there is some size overlap between black and grizzly bears.

Black bear droppings are humanlike in shape, although they are usually larger in diameter, up to 1¾ inches. Fragments of food the animals have been feeding on are usually visible in scats such as wild cherry pits, beech nut hulls, apple peels, or grass. Droppings are normally black or brown in color, but are sometimes white or gray, depending upon diet. Raccoon-size droppings with distinct bear size dung are a sure sign a sow and at least one cub have been in the area. When eating berries, scats will sometimes be fluidy and shapeless, or form flat patties.

There are a number of other signs left by black bears to look for, most of which consist of feeding sign. Black bears sometimes do a lot of damage to food-bearing trees, often breaking limbs and sometimes breaking the trunks of small to medium-sized trees to get at the fruits or berries they contain. Trees that blacks climb usually exhibit gouges in the bark from claws. Underlying wood will be visible in claw marks that are not very old. Old claw marks heal over and turn black. Claw marks from black bears can be seen most often on aspen, oak, beech, apple, and cherry trees.

Blacks are fond of insects and while looking for them will roll logs and

Bear scat varies in color, depending on the animal's diet.

A ''bear tree'' with bear hair visible on broken limbs.

The bark of this large beech tree bears the scars of many claw marks from bears.

rocks over, rip rotted logs and stumps apart, or dig hornet nests out of the ground. These animals are capable of moving large logs and rocks, which may be found later scarred or scratched by claws.

A habit bears in some western states have during the spring that has gotten them into trouble with timber companies is ripping bark from the bases of evergreen trees to get at the pulpy sapwood. In some cases, the bark is removed all the way around the trunk, girdling the trees, which kills them. The animals also feed heavily on oats and corn in the fall, to the displeasure of affected farmers.

Evidence of black bears can also be found on trees that may be used as territorial markers and are referred to as bear trees. Small to medium size evergreens are often used as bear trees in the upper midwest and Canada. The tops of these trees are usually broken, but left hanging, and limbs are broken, too. Blacks normally scratch themselves on broken limbs. Large trees are used by blacks to scratch themselves on and claw in some parts of the country. Claw marks are generally as high as the animal that made them can reach. Man-made signs and buildings, most of which are abandoned, are chewed or clawed by black bears, too.

Observant hikers, campers, or hunters may notice bear hairs on the

A pair of black bear cubs in den above ground. Bark from dead tree they are laying next to was scraped off by their mother to provide bedding.

Another black bear excavated a hole under this stump for its winter den.

undersides of fallen or low-growing trees in addition to those left on bear trees. These animals frequently walk under fallen or leaning trees and limbs that are 2 or 3 feet off the ground and leave some hairs on the underside in the process. Hairs should be especially noticeable on limb stubs pointing downward.

Still another bear sign are trails, usually established in areas where the animals come to feed on a regular basis. Grass and other low-growing vegetation is flattened on bear trails from repeated trampling by flat feet. At garbage dumps where black bears use the same trails to reach it year after year, paths will be worn down to bare soil. Where these trails enter thickets, they usually form tunnels through them, about 3 feet high.

Beds of black bears are not often seen because they are generally located in dense cover. Bear beds are roughly the size and shape of deer beds, although they tend to be more circular. Their shape can usually be determined from flattened vegetation or a shallow depression in the soil. Any hairs in beds can help determine what animal used it.

Most of the winter is spent in dens. A variety of sites are used for dens such as caves, brushpiles, and hollow trees. Some black bears simply make nests out in the open where they spend the winter, and snow covers them as it falls. One Michigan bear simply curled up on top of a muskrat house for the winter, another slept in an abandoned beaver house, and a third one curled up in a hole it dug under a stump. In Smoky Mountains National Park, and other areas in the south, black bears have been found to den in tree cavities well above the ground.

Black bears have a wider range than other bears. They are most common in Canada and Alaska, plus western states such as Washington, Oregon, Montana, Wyoming, Idaho, Colorado, Utah, Arizona, New Mexico, and northern California. In the eastern United States they are found in Maine, New Hampshire, Vermont, Massachusetts, New York, and Pennsylvania. They occupy parts of the Carolinas, Virginias, Tennessee, Arkansas, Georgia, and Florida in the south. Their stronghold in the midwest are the northern portions of Michigan, Wisconsin, and Minnesota.

Grizzly bears like this one have humps on their backs at the shoulders.

Track of a grizzly with claw marks prominent. (Photograph courtesy of Lloyd Bare.)

These animals are secretive, spending a lot of time in thick swamps and rugged mountainous terrain. However, they also spend a lot of time in stands of hardwoods, especially where mast-bearing trees are present. Despite their secretive nature, blacks sometimes reside relatively close to towns where the habitat is suitable, which is of little consequence since these animals are not as dangerous as commonly thought. Wild black bears usually go out of their way to avoid contact with people.

Grizzlies and Brown Bears

Grizzly tracks are 4 to 6 inches wide across front pads and hind feet measure 7 to 12 inches in length. Front feet of adult brown bears vary from 8 to 9 inches in width and hind foot prints are 15 to 16 inches long.

Most grizzlies are brown in color, but can vary from blond to dark chocolate, and have a distinct hump on their shoulders. Grizzlies weigh from 300 to 600 pounds on the average, with females at the lower end of the scale and brown bears attain weights from 500 to 1,200 pounds, with heavier weights on record. One of the reasons brown bears attain the size they do is a rich diet of fish. They eat spawning salmon during the summer, although grizzlies also feed on salmon.

The brown bear's range is restricted to an area along the west coast of Alaska and parts of the Yukon and British Columbia nearest the state. Grizzlies have a much wider distribution, found throughout Alaska, the Yukon, British Columbia, and into Alberta and the Northwest Territories. In the lower forty-eight states, grizzly bears are concentrated in an area near the borders of Montana, Wyoming, and Idaho, plus a portion of northern Montana, Idaho, and Washington.

Animals on a fruit or fish diet may leave soft, flat manure piles. When eating grass or meat, droppings are more characteristic of bears, being 2 or more inches in diameter.

Bear trails are common along salmon spawning streams and other locations the animals frequent. These trails usually have staggered depressions at regular intervals worn over time by bears constantly placing their feet in the same place.

The grizzly bear's long claws are well suited for digging, and they put them to good use unearthing roots, tubers, ground squirrels, and marmots. Large areas are sometimes dug up by these animals in their search for food. Tracks are usually visible in excavated soil.

While the grizzly's long claws are perfect for digging, they are poorly designed for climbing. Consequently, adult grizzlies seldom climb trees, unless limbs are spaced closely enough on a tree trunk for them to use like rungs of a ladder. Young grizzly bears are better able to climb trees than adults.

Grizzlies mark trees in much the same manner as black bears, rubbing and clawing them to leave hair and scratch marks. A number of animals visit most bear trees. As might be guessed, beds from these bears are large in size. The animals sometimes rake together moss and other debris to lie on. Natural cavities are used as dens or suitable winter quarters are excavated. These dens are usually well hidden.

Grizzly and brown bears call a variety of habitat home from the rain

Deep gouges in the bark of this wild cherry tree identify the culprit as a bear.

forests along the coast of Alaska to the open tundra. In the lower forty-eight, remaining grizzlies occupy remote, rugged, mountainous terrain for the most part.

Polar Bears

Few people are likely to see polar bear tracks, which are most often visible in snow on open ice in arctic regions where the animals hunt for seals. The feet are hairy, obscuring details of pads in prints. Since there is little overlap between grizzly and polar bear range, and polar bear tracks are distinctive, there is not much chance their prints would be mistaken for those of any other bear. The southern edge of the polar bear's range barely reaches into the northern fringes of Alaska and Canada, and goes way north from there. These all white bears range in weight from 750 to over 1,000 pounds with weights over 2,000 pounds on record.

10

Deer

UNLIKE OTHER ANIMALS discussed so far, deer only have two toes on each foot, which form hooves. Each toe makes up half of a hoof. Front hooves are larger than those on hind feet. Deer tracks made by a walking animal may resemble an upside-down heart, with the bottom of the heart being the tips of the toes, if toes are close together. And, of course, there is a line running down the middle of the heart-shaped tracks that marks the inner edge of each toe.

When trotting or running, toes will be spread and small marks from dew claws, which can be considered a deer's heels, often appear directly behind each toe. Impressions from dew claws may also appear in walking tracks made in mud, soft sand, or snow an inch or more deep. The dew claws simply increase the surface area of feet for added support. Dew claws are further from toes on hind feet than they are on front feet.

This characteristic can be helpful in differentiating between front and back feet in running deer tracks. Whitetail deer characteristically leave imprints from hind feet in front of forefeet when running. Mule deer and blacktail deer, on the other hand, leave running prints with front feet ahead of hind feet. The reason for this is differences in their gait.

Whitetails run like most other animals with their front feet striking the ground as they bring hind feet forward to touch down ahead of them to kick off with a powerful forward bound or leap. Muleys and blacktails, which are closely related, generally keep their legs stiff when running and bounce from one spot to the next like they have pogo sticks for legs. The only circumstance under which mule deer and whitetail tracks can reliably be distinguished from one another is when they are running, due to this fundamental difference in how they run.

The ability to tell the difference between the tracks of different species of deer is not necessary in most areas because there is not a lot of overlap in their ranges. Where two species do share the same range, the different animals normally occupy distinct types of habitat. In some western states where both mule deer and whitetails are found such as Montana and Wyoming, whitetails spend much of their time in lowland river bottoms and agricultural areas with woodlots. Muleys inhabit timbered slopes and meadows at higher elevations, for the most part.

Track patterns left by running deer may appear in one of two forms. The four footprints are sometimes bunched together, with both front and rear feet slightly offset from one another rather than side by side. Prints of front feet may be closer together than those of hind feet in patterns left by mule deer or blacktails. A more elongated running track pattern exhibits tracks of individual feet farther apart, almost in a line. However, each print is usually to the right or left of the center of the track pattern.

The length of footprints in running tracks, including dew claws, ranges from 3½ to 4½ inches for most adult deer. Tracks of walking deer range from 2½ to more than 3 inches in length. Keep in mind that there is a tremendous variation in track size among deer from one part of the country to another, even within the same species. Whitetails tend to be smaller in the southern portion of the United States, for instance, than in the north.

Two of the smallest subspecies of whitetails are found in the south. The key deer is the smallest and lives in the Florida Keys. Coues deer inhabit desert regions in parts of the southwestern United States. Tracks made by adults of these subspecies may be similar in size to prints made by fawns from Wisconsin, Pennsylvania, New York, Maine, or Michigan in the fall.

It is not unusual to see the tracks of two or more deer traveling together at any time of the year. In fact, the animals are sometimes seen in groups or herds, especially in feeding areas. One or two sets of small tracks with those of a noticeably larger animal are obviously made by a doe and her fawns. Two or more sets of adult-size prints may be those of a buck and does, especially during late fall breeding seasons, or simply does traveling together.

When deer travel over the same route time and time again, or many animals follow the same course, trails develop. Heavily used trails are usually

Deer tracks are heart-shaped like this one sometimes when the animals are walking. This print was made by a whitetail.

Mule deer track. This print looks different from many whitetail tracks, although many mule deer tracks look like those of whitetails and vice-versa. (Photograph courtesy of Chuck Adams.)

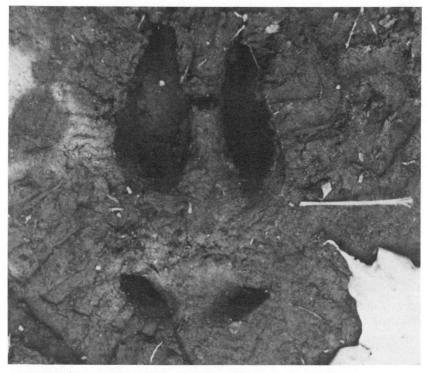

Running deer track with dew claw marks visible at bottom of print.

void of vegetation, and numerous tracks can be seen in them. These may lead to favored feeding areas or mark migration routes used by some deer during late fall into winter and spring. The course of less used trails can usually be determined by a line of scuffed leaves or flattened vegetation. Trails are easiest to see in sand and snow.

One fairly reliable way to tell the tracks of a buck from those of a doe, if there is an inch of snow or less on the ground, is to look for drag marks. Bucks do not generally lift their feet as high as does do, dragging their feet in the snow from one step to the next. When snow gets deeper, deer of either sex may drag their feet.

Big bucks make tracks that are both longer and wider than those of most does. So an exceptionally large track like the one I measured last fall that was 4 inches long and 3¾ inches wide across the rear of the print, are often made by bucks. However, this is only true in areas where big bucks live. Bucks in some locations with heavy hunting pressure seldom live longer than 2½ years, not long enough to attain large size. Does in the same area may live longer and grow larger, leaving tracks bigger than those of most bucks.

Running track pattern of deer. Whitetails run so that prints from hind feet appear in front of those of front feet. It is the opposite for mule and blacktail deer.

Measurements of the feet of more than 100 blacktail deer from Oregon showed that adult bucks definitely do have wider and longer feet than adult does. The feet of adult bucks averaged 73 millimeters or 2.874 inches in length, with the shortest being 71 millimeters or 2.795 inches. Adult doe feet averaged 66 millimeters or 2.598 inches, with 68.5 millimeters or 2.697 inches the longest, so there was no overlap. There was some overlap in foot size among yearling bucks and does, but the length of feet among males averaged longer even in that age class (68 millimeters or 2.677 inches versus 64 millimeters or 2.52 inches).

The same was true for width of feet measured one-third of the way back from tips of toes. Feet of yearling bucks averaged wider, 15 millimeters or .591 inches versus 13.8 millimeters or .543 inches. There was a clearcut difference in width of feet among adult bucks and does, averaging 17 millimeters or .669 inches for bucks and 14 millimeters or .551 inches for does. The widest adult doe track measured 14.5 millimeters or .571 inches and the narrowest buck foot was 16.5 millimeters or .65 inches.

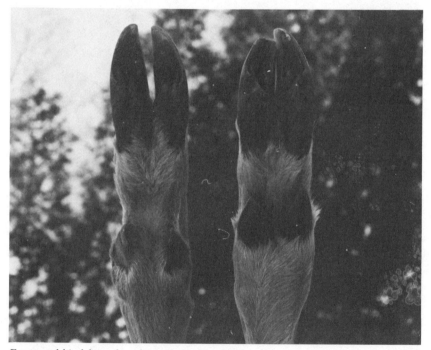

Front and hind feet of a whitetail. Notice that dew claws are further from hooves on hind foot.

This sample also showed that foot size of both bucks and does were comparable as fawns. The same information probably applies to whitetail and mule deer, too, but it would be better if similar studies had been done of their feet to confirm it.

If a track is thought to have been made by a mature buck due to its size, one way to confirm those suspicions, at least during fall and early winter months, is to follow the animal's tracks and look for other signs. A blanket of snow on the ground is necessary to make this possible, of course. Look for locations where the deer stopped to feed on items close to or on the ground. In locations where acorns and other types of nuts are found, the animals will paw up leaves on the ground, sometimes in large patches, to get at the nuts. Antler tines from bucks with decent size antlers (six points or better) will sometimes leave impressions in the snow as they feed on acorns. All tines will not necessarily show in the snow. Small antlered bucks usually will not leave any marks in the snow from their headgear.

Black bears and raccoons will also paw through patches of leaves like deer to feed on nuts. So when seeing this type of sign, especially when no snow is on the ground, look for droppings or tracks in the soil to better determine what was responsible for the activity.

Deer also graze on grass or eat fallen apples in openings or fields where these items are found, and signs of antlers may sometimes be discovered in the snow at these locations. The first time I noticed round holes in the snow from antler tips on either side of a spot where a buck had been feeding, the animal had been eating fallen apples. Two or three punctures were visible on each side and they were widespread, so it appeared as though the buck had a respectable set of antlers. I followed the animal in an effort to find out just how big they were, but never did get a glimpse of its head.

Deer are browsers, too, breaking off the tips of limbs, saplings, and low-growing stems. Look for evidence of tines in the snow where a deer browses on stems growing close to the ground. Because deer do not have teeth on top in the front of their mouths, they must break off bits of woody browse rather than biting them off cleanly. As a result, ragged edges will be visible on the ends of plants, brush, and trees where deer have browsed. Rabbits clip twigs off cleanly, at a slant, where they feed. Refer to photos in this chapter and the one on rabbits for a comparison.

There are other signs that can confirm whether tracks were made by a buck in the fall. That is the time of year when the "rut" or breeding season takes place. Mature bucks leave two types of signs in conjunction with the rut—antler rubbings and ground scrapes. Antler rubs are made on trees of various sizes, but most often on saplings. Bucks rake their antlers along the trunks of selected trees, sometimes so aggressively that the sapling is broken.

The bark is rubbed off on tree trunks worked over by bucks, some of it

A deer bit off tip of branch in the center of photo. Notice how rough the break is compared to the clean cut made by rabbits and hares.

If tracking a deer and its trail leads to a freshly rubbed sapling like this one with bark on top of the snow, the tracks are those of a buck.

left hanging in ragged strips. Light-colored inner wood on fresh rubs can usually be spotted from some distance away. Antler rubs made by deer are normally only a foot or two off the ground. Bits of bark and wood can generally be seen at the bases of rubbed trees. Rubs on full-fledged trees are made by bucks with large antlers, as a rule. Since the bases of both beams are rubbed on trees, the antlers have to be at least as wide as the damaged tree to fit around it.

Scrapes are patches of ground, most often located underneath an overhanging limb, that bucks paw free of leaves and other debris exposing bare soil. Bucks often leave scent on the overhanging branch by nibbling on it or rubbing a secretion from a gland at the corners of their eyes on them. Bucks may also attack these branches with their antlers. As a result, many such limbs are broken and left hanging or broken off entirely and can be seen laying on the ground in the scrape or near it. Bucks often urinate in scrapes, which can vary in size, once they are complete. Tracks may also be visible in scrapes.

Rubs and scrapes are sometimes found together, or at least in the same vicinity, but not always. Scrapes help bucks and receptive does get together during the rut when the time is right. Once does are ready to be bred, they visit a scrape to leave their scent. For this reason, bucks usually check their scrapes (each animal makes a series of these markers) on a regular basis. When a scrape has been visited by a doe, the buck trails her from there until he finds her.

All deer make rubs and scrapes, but whitetails make more scrapes than mule deer or blacktails. In fact, scrapes are not as important to mule deer as whitetails. Due to the whitetail buck's habit of revisiting scrapes during the rut, anyone who finds a series of them in a small area can usually see the animal that made them by waiting in the vicinity.

Deer tracks that lead up to a freshly made rub or scrape are those of a buck. If they are fresh, rubbed bark and pawed soil will be on top of the snow. A second set of tracks leading to a scrape could be those of a doe, or of another buck in the area. Bucks will visit scrapes made by other males, and may even add their scent to them.

Deer beds are oval-shaped depressions in grass, moss, leaves, or snow where the animals lay down to chew their cud or rest. Animals that are traveling together may bed down in the same locality. Large and small beds together usually represent those of a doe and fawns. Marks from antlers can sometimes be seen at the head end of beds in the snow made by bucks. During the rut, the tracks of a buck will frequently lead to the beds of other deer in their search of does ready to be bred.

If one rutting buck encounters another of equal size, a fight sometimes takes place, and the evidence of such a contest is unmistakable. The ground

Whitetail droppings.

Mule deer pellets. (Photograph courtesy of Kent and Donna Dannen.)

will usually be trampled, with turf torn up, trees and bushes will be knocked over, and clumps of hair will be visible on the ground. I saw signs left by a pair of fighting whitetails last fall that were impressive. It appeared as though their antlers may have been locked for a time because there was a continuous trail of devastation for a good 50 yards where they pushed, pulled, and shoved one another. The antlers of fighting bucks sometimes become inseparably locked and they die.

Beds in fields usually mark locations where animals laid down to chew their cud or rest during hours of darkness. Beds in thick cover are usually daytime resting places. An accumulation of deer beds in a location that has been used over a period of time, some old, some fresh, is indicative of a preferred bedding area. Anyone interested in intercepting deer between bedding and feeding areas should post as close to bedding areas as possible without alerting the animals in the evening. Persons who beat deer to bedding areas in the morning stand a good chance of seeing the animals when they arrive. When waiting for deer it is important to be positioned so the wind does not carry your scent in the direction deer will be coming from. Deer that smell people generally will not show themselves.

Deer may urinate and/or defecate in their beds when they arise at their leisure. Urine marks made by does are usually smaller in circumference and between or slightly behind rear hoofprints. Urine from bucks falls further forward and may be splattered over a wider area because they often urinate over glands located on hind legs, at least in the fall. Drops of urine can sometimes be seen in the snow between tracks made by a walking buck.

Deer droppings consist of groupings of pellets of a half-inch to an inch in length that are usually black or brown in color, but they may have a greenish cast. Deer pellets are cylindrical in shape with rounded ends, as a rule, but one end of some pellets may be concave with the other possessing a nipple-shaped projection. In the summer, deer scats may appear as individual clumps of fecal material rather than pellets.

Deer hair is another sign the animals sometimes leave, although it is not one of the more important ones. Long, brownish, hollow deer hairs can be found in narrow places along trails where they rub or bump against trees and brush. Hairs are also left on strands of barbed wire where the animals crawl under fences. Deer hair can serve as an important sign for hunters that an animal was hit, if found on the ground where the deer was standing when shot at. Both bullets and arrows cut hair from deer when striking them, even though there may be no blood at that point.

Concentrations of bleached, white antlers shed by bucks are sometimes seen in locations where deer winter, especially the open terrain mule deer favor. Deer are usually only abundant in these areas during the winter when deep snows push them down from higher elevations. Most bucks shed their

A pair of whitetail deer. Note large brown tails with white borders and the underside is all white.

Both mule deer like this one and blacktails grow antlers on which the tines commonly fork. (Photograph courtesy of Montana Department of Fish and Game.)

A blacktail deer. Tail is black and narrower than the whitetail. (Photograph courtesy of Chuck Adams.)

antlers during the winter, but some may lose them late in the fall or retain them until spring. Healthy bucks usually have antlers longer than under-nourished or injured males. Mule deer antlers characteristically have branched tines. Typical whitetail antlers have tines that do not branch, but nontypical antlers exhibited by some whitetails do have branched tines.

Another deer sign common in wintering areas with too many deer are browse lines. These distinct lines visible on trees and other vegetation are created by the animals eating everything edible within reach.

In appearance, the three major types of deer under discussion here are easy to tell apart. Whitetails have large tails that are white on the underside and brown on top. When alarmed, these deer raise their tails and they resemble a white flag waving as they run. This serves as a warning to other animals in the vicinity.

Mule deer tails are much narrower than those of whitetails and conse-quently, do not cover their rump. The tails are black at the tip, with the rest being white. Blacktails are a subspecies of mule deer, and as their name implies, tails are black on top, not on the underside. The tails of blacktails are similar in size and shape to those of whitetails.

All of these deer have coats that are brown to gray during fall, winter, and spring months. Summer coats are reddish brown. Whitetails average between 100 to 150 pounds, with smaller subspecies usually weighing under 100 pounds. Some enormous whitetails have been recorded that weighed more than 300 pounds. Average weights of blacktails are similar to those for whitetails. Muleys average between 150 and 200 pounds, with larger animals reaching weights of 300 to 400 pounds or more.

Blacktail deer are only found along the west coast of North America, with sitka blacktails found in southern Alaska and into British Columbia. Columbian blacktails are distributed along the coast of British Columbia, Washington, Oregon, and northern California. Mule deer are found in all western states and western Canada. The eastern limit of their range is on a line with western portions of Nebraska and the Dakotas.

Whitetail deer reside in all of the lower forty-eight states, but few are found in California, Nevada, and Utah. Parts of other states such as northern Arizona, western Colorado, southwestern Wyoming, and southern Idaho are also without whitetails. All of southern Canada, with the exception of most of British Columbia, is home to whitetails, as well.

11

Elk, Moose, and Caribou

Elk and Moose

The tracks of elk and moose are similar to those of deer since the animals are closely related, except elk and moose tracks are much larger. Elk tracks measure 4 inches in length, with some variation either way, and usually have more rounded toes than those of moose, which measure 5 inches or more in length. The length of running moose tracks may be as much as 10 inches, including the dew claws, with running elk tracks shorter.

Footprints of elk can be confused with those of cattle at times, although adult cattle usually leave tracks slightly larger and more rounded than those of adult elk. Young cattle make tracks intermediate in size, about 3 inches, between those of adult and calf elk (2 inches). Look for droppings if in doubt as to which animal made tracks. Elk scat may resemble those of cattle (flat patties) in the summer, but are much smaller, only 5 or 6 inches in diameter. However, elk scats are often in pellet form.

Elk pellets are elongated like those of deer and can be rounded on the ends or concave and pointed. Scat from elk measure ¾ of an inch to twice that in some cases. Moose pellets are sometimes shaped the same as those of elk, but may resemble large marbles in shape, and are generally an inch

A bull elk with high antlers, dark neck, and light rump.

Elk tracks, which are much larger than those of deer and usually smaller than those of moose. Elk tracks normally exhibit rounded toes.

Tracks of a walking elk.

Another form of elk droppings. (Photograph courtesy of Leonard Lee Rue III.)

A bull moose with palmate antlers.

to 1¾ inches long. Moose will also void larger quantities of scat than elk, averaging a quart, in one location.

Moose commonly travel alone, although a cow may have a calf with her. And during the fall rut, the tracks of a bull and cow may be seen together. However, moose are sometimes gregarious with groups often visible in small areas. I have seen two or three bulls and a cow together in Wyoming. Elk are herd animals, but bulls sometimes wander off on their own.

Elk are grazers primarily, so look for their tracks and droppings in meadows surrounded by timber. When they do browse, willow is a preferred species. Patches above timberline are most often visited by elk during the summer and early fall. Aspen bark is also eaten during winter. Elk gouge out pieces of bark from tree trunks with their canine teeth. Old scars from this type of feeding activity blacken. Light-colored inner wood can be seen where bark was recently removed.

Moose chew bark from aspen trees, too, so either animal may be responsible if both are present where this sign is noticed. I have also seen where a moose ate bark from maple trees. Willows browsed by moose frequently have stems broken by the animals as they pull the tops down to get at tender tips in tops. Other species of small trees moose browse on may be damaged in a similar fashion. Moose commonly feed on water plants during summer months, so look for their tracks along shores of lakes, ponds, or rivers at that time of year. In the winter, moose browse on some evergreen trees such as balsams, sometimes leaving noticeable browse lines.

Like deer, elk and moose rub their antlers on trees during the fall prior to and during the rut. Both elk and moose rubs are on larger trees than deer use and higher off the ground than deer normally rub. Males of both species sometimes fight during the rut. Moose antlers sometimes lock like those of deer, and then the animals die.

There are a few moose where I live in upper Michigan, although they are abundant on Isle Royale in Lake Superior, but their primary range is further north in all of Canada and Alaska. Moose are common in Maine and more numerous in Minnesota (the northern part) than Michigan. The animals also range into Vermont and New Hampshire. Western states that have moose are Utah, Colorado, Wyoming, Idaho, Montana, and Washington. Shira's moose, the smallest subspecies, reside in western states. Canadian moose are larger, and Alaskan moose are the largest subspecies.

The smaller subspecies of moose range in weight from 800 to at least 1,200 pounds. Alaskan moose reach weights of 1,800 pounds.

In weight, elk are lighter than moose, but there is some overlap. Six hundred to 1,000 pounds is the weight scale for elk. The elk's primary range includes Montana, Idaho, Wyoming, Colorado, Utah, New Mexico, Arizona, Washington, Oregon, and California, in the United States. Pockets of the

Prints left by a cow and a calf moose. Note the difference in size between the prints of the calf and the cow. (Photograph courtesy of Robert Janke.)

Bull moose track with a three-inch shotgun shell for size comparison. Note how pointed the toes are.

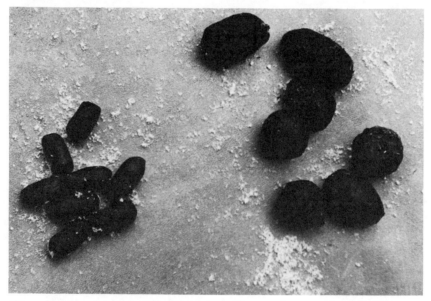

Elk and moose scat compared. The moose pellets are larger and some of them are rounded.

Shed moose antler at the base of a rubbed tree. Note that the height of the rub is much higher than a deer would rub its antlers. (Photograph courtesy of Cathy Rezabeck.)

animals are also found in South Dakota, Texas, Arkansas, Virginia, and Michigan. In Canada, they are distributed in parts of Manitoba, Saskatchewan, Alberta, and British Columbia.

Elk and moose beds are much larger than those made by deer, with vegetation and snow being flattened under the animals where they lay. Beds may be found singly or in clusters. Both animals also make and use wallows in conjunction with the breeding season. Elk wallow in moist, black soil along the edges of meadows, and moose do the same although the location may be different. The animals often urinate in wallows then roll in the odorous mud.

Due to their size, these animals are not likely to be mistaken for anything else. Moose are dark brown to black. Bulls have palmate or flat antlers and an appendage hanging under their chins called bells. Their antlers are shed annually.

The bodies of elk are tan in color, with much darker, longer hair on the neck. Their rumps are light in color, cream to yellow, and sometimes give the animals' presence away because this part of their anatomy contrasts with their surroundings and is easy to spot. Mature bulls grow tall antlers with long tines, which are shed every year and replaced with a new set. While developing, all antlers of members of the deer family are covered with velvet. The velvet is shed early in the fall, exposing hardened antlers.

Caribou

Caribou tracks are unlike those of any other member of the deer family. The sharply curved toes form two halves of an incomplete circle. Prints would be perfectly circular if toes came together, but there is usually wide spacing between the toes, more so in the center of tracks than at tips of toes. Dew claws are almost always visible in caribou tracks, even when the animals are walking.

These animals spend a lot of time on wet, spongy ground, and the design of their hooves help support their weight when walking or running. Many caribou inhabit treeless terrain or tundra in Canada and Alaska where their primary food is lichen, a type of moss, although they also graze on grasses and browse on woody plants. One subspecies of caribou, the woodland variety, is more often found in association with forested areas than their relatives.

Caribou are nomadic, traveling long distances during the course of a year, especially on spring and fall migrations. Their migration routes are marked by heavily used trails that wind their way across the tundra. Once snow covers the ground, caribou dig down through it, sometimes more than a foot, to reach lichen and grass it covers. I have seen signs left by whitetail deer doing the same thing to reach grass, as well as apples.

A small group of barren ground caribou. Note the large antlers characteristic of bulls. (Photograph courtesy of Leonard Lee Rue III.)

A caribou track. (Photograph courtesy of Chuck Adams.)

Scat left by these animals is not an important sign. It closely resembles dung deposited by other members of the deer family, as well as sheep.

Both male and female caribou grow antlers, which is unusual among members of the deer family. In fact, caribou are the only antlered animals in North America with females that grow antlers, although this characteristic is common among horned big game. The difference between antlers and horns is that antlers are shed annually. Horns are not shed, and they grow continuously as a result.

Antlers grown by cow caribou are generally spindly and small. Mature bulls grow large antlers with long beams that are sometimes palmate on the ends like those of moose. Auxiliary beams often project upward near the base of main beams and flat "shovels" may also extend forward from the base of antlers. Caribou antlers, like the animals themselves, are different.

Caribou are also known as reindeer, which most children and adults would recognize as the animals that are supposed to pull Santa Claus' sleigh on Christmas. The bodies of these animals are dark brown, with much lighter-colored hair on their necks. They also have white rump patches. Barren ground caribou generally weigh between 300 and 400 pounds, but the woodland subspecies weigh upwards of 600 pounds or more.

The range of caribou includes much of Canada and Alaska, with the animals being absent from southern portions of most provinces.

12

Other Hooved Animals

Pronghorn Antelope

The tracks of pronghorn antelope are similar to those of deer, although they tend to be wider at the rear than deer tracks and the inside of toes are slightly concave toward the tips. This results in the front of the toes being spread wider in antelope tracks than is typical of deer tracks. One distinct difference between deer and pronghorn feet is antelope do not have dew claws, so they will not be visible in running antelope tracks.

Pronghorn tracks average just under 3 inches to a little more than 3 inches in length. Antelope themselves are often easier to see than their tracks because they occupy open plains and grasslands where they can be spotted a long way off. The animals' upper bodies are brown with white on the rump, sides, chest, and throat. Their white markings normally stand out against their surroundings. Antelope are often seen in herds. The animals range between 80 and 125 pounds or more.

Both male and female pronghorns grow black horns that have curled ends and prongs on each horn, usually closer to the bases than tips. Horns grown by does seldom grow as long as those of bucks, with 3 to 4 inches

A small group of pronghorn antelope with a buck on the left and does on the right.

Track of a pronghorn antelope. Note how narrow the toes are at the tips and wide at the rear. (Photograph courtesy of Chuck Adams.)

being normal. The horns of bucks can be as much as 20 inches long, but are usually less. Antelope do not shed their horns each year like deer do, although the outer sheath is replaced annually. The inner core of horns remain intact continuously.

In locations where both mule deer and antelope occupy the same habitat, their tracks can be confused, especially where clear prints are not visible. Scats of antelope also resemble those of mule deer. However, a type of sign characteristic of pronghorns associated with their scat is a depression pawed in the ground for depositing both droppings and urine. These are referred to as scrapes, but do not have any connection with mating like those made by whitetail deer.

The distribution of pronghorn antelope is more spotty than deer, due primarily to the occurrence of their preferred habitat. They are found in most western states and into the Dakotas, with good numbers in states such as Wyoming, Montana, Colorado, and South Dakota. In Canada, these animals are found in parts of Alberta and Saskatchewan just north of the United States border.

Mountain Goats

Mountain goats make tracks that are shaped like a square. Prints are about as wide at the front as they are at the back, although there is generally an indentation where the toes are separated at the front. Adult goat footprints average more than 3 inches in length, with 3½ inches typical.

Like pronghorns, mountain goats can be easier to see than their tracks in areas where they are found. They usually occupy rocky, mountainous regions. The animals are totally white and have short, black horns that come to a point. Both sexes grow horns, which are not shed, and the horns of females can be as long as those of males. Patches of long white, shaggy hair they shed during the summer can sometimes be found on trees and brush in areas they occupy.

The scats of mountain goats are more irregularly shaped than those of deer when in pellet form, but they do resemble deer droppings in some cases. However, many times goat pellets tend to be more bell shaped than those of deer, with pointed tops and flat, widened bottoms. Droppings may also be round like marbles. Summer dung may appear as conglomerations of pellets clinging together or soft masses of feces that harden when dry.

Mountain goat beds are usually located on slopes where they have good visibility, but may also be seen in caves and other protected areas where the animals go to escape inclement weather. These animals average much larger than deer and antelope, with billies (males) attaining weights of up to 300 pounds. These wild goats are distributed from Washington State northward

A white-coated mountain goat.

Square-shaped mountain goat tracks. (Photograph courtesy of Chuck Adams.)

Droppings from a mountain goat that are basically circular in shape. (Photograph courtesy of Leonard Lee Rue III.)

through British Columbia and into parts of the Yukon and Alaska. They also range from Idaho and Montana into British Columbia and Alberta. Scattered populations of the animals brought about through releases are in Colorado, Wyoming, and South Dakota.

Wild Sheep

The tracks of wild sheep are similar to those of mountain goats, being squared, although the inner edges of toes on goats tend to be straighter than those of sheep. The inner edges of the toes of sheep are slightly concave and this shows in some tracks. Tracks of the front feet of sheep range between 3 and 3½ inches, with back footprints shorter.

There are two species of wild sheep—*bighorns* and *Dalls*. Bighorns are generally tan to brown in color with light-colored rumps. They are commonly found in mountainous regions of the western United States and Canada, but a smaller variety referred to as desert bighorns, reside in desert regions in the southwestern United States southward into Mexico. Desert Bighorns may attain weights of 200 pounds, usually less, while some of their alpine relatives reach weights of 300 pounds.

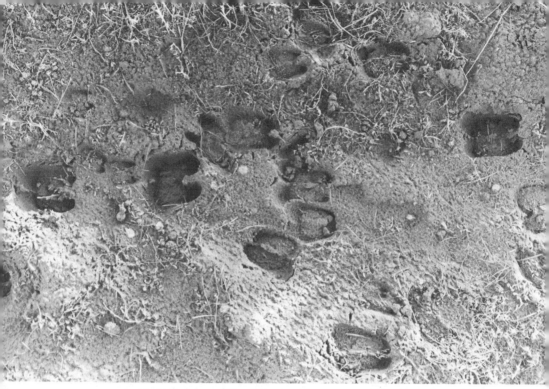

Dall sheep tracks. (Photograph courtesy of Chuck Adams.)

A mature bighorn ram.

Dall sheep are pure white, but there are color variations with some black to gray evident. A subspecies called Stone sheep are gray to black in color, with the exception of white rumps, bellies, and backs of legs. Dall sheep average smaller than bighorns, with weights in the 200-pound range, give or take 25 pounds, common.

Both rams and ewes grow horns, but the ewes' horns are pointed and curved backward. Mature rams grow massive horns that curl back around to or past their eyes.

Sheep scats closely resemble those of mountain goats, tending to be bell shaped when in pellet form. Bighorns and Dalls have a habit of using the same beds, which are depressions 6 inches to a foot deep and bare soil, repeatedly as long as they remain in one area. The edges of favored beds are often lined with droppings. Sheep urinate in the beds themselves.

Bighorn sheep reside in portions of most western states in mountain ranges and in Alberta and British Columbia. The Dall sheep range includes northern British Columbia, northwestern Yukon and Alaska's mountain ranges. Representatives of the Stone sheep subspecies are most common in northern British Columbia and southern Yukon.

Buffalo

Another hooved animal of the open plains is the buffalo. Their tracks resemble those of domestic cattle and can be confused with them, although buffalo tracks are generally larger. The prints of adult buffaloes measure 5 inches or more, both in length and width. Cow tracks are usually less than 5 inches in length.

Tracks left by buffaloes are circular in shape and could pass for those of a horse if it were not for the two toes. Horses only have one toe on each foot. The outside of each toe on the feet of buffalo are semicircular and the insides are concave.

Buffaloes are brown in color with horns that curve to the sides and upward. Both bulls and cows have horns. The animals weigh between 900 and 1,800 pounds, but some bulls are heavier and some cows lighter.

Dung from buffalos look exactly like cow patties and can be confused for the same. Other sign made by these animals include tree rubs and wallows. Even though buffalos spend a lot of time on open grasslands, they also enter stands of trees, usually pines. Trunks of trees where buffalo roam are rubbed and gouged with horns, forming a light band of scarred bark. Long, brown, kinky buffalo hairs are usually visible on rubs.

Wallows are enlarged beds worn down to the soil where buffalos roll in the dust. A number of wallows may be seen close together. The large patches of bare soil stand out against green grass making them easy to see. Tree rubs

A bull buffalo in Custer State Park, South Dakota.

Buffalo tracks, which are basically circular in shape. (Photograph courtesy of Leonard Lee Rue III.)

Buffalo scat.

A javelina or peccary.

Javelina track. (Photograph courtesy of Chuck Adams.)

and wallows are numerous in South Dakota's Custer State Park, which has one of the largest herds of free-roaming buffalos in the country. Buffalo herds are also located in southern Oklahoma, eastern Utah, northwest Wyoming, southeast Montana, plus a couple of locations in Alberta and Alaska.

Wild Pigs

There are a couple of varieties of wild pigs in the United States—small peccaries or javelina and much larger hogs of European origin released in some states. Javelina tracks are an inch to 1½ inches in length. Their toes are blunt and rounded, which shows in prints, so they should not be confused with small deer tracks. Peccary only have one dew claw on hind feet and the normal two on front feet, but they seldom register in tracks.

Dew claws are a very important part of the tracks of larger pigs though. In fact, the dew claws on other hogs are prominent enough to be considered additional toes. Dew claws are located to either side of the normal two toes forming hooves, rather than directly behind them, and are more pointed than on other hooved animals. Imprints from dew claws routinely show in pig

Javelina have fed on this cactus. (Photograph courtesy of Chuck Adams.)

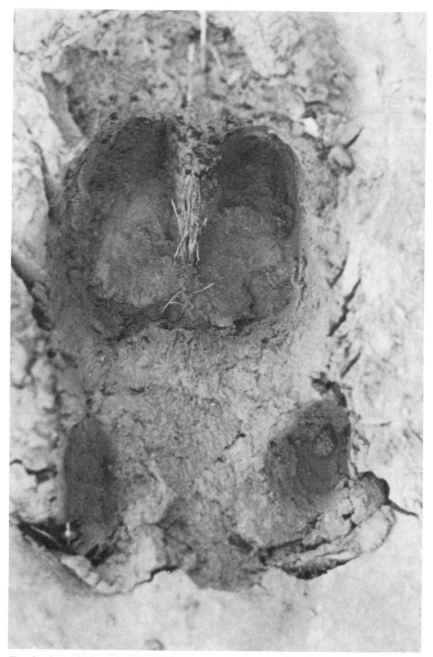

Track of a wild boar. Note the rounded toes and prominent dew claw marks. (Photograph courtesy of Chuck Adams.)

tracks, behind and to the sides of hoofprints. Toes that form hooves are normally wide spread with a *U-* or *V*-shaped notch between them.

Javelina are a peppery gray to black in color with stiff bristles for hair. They average from 30 to 45 pounds or more in weight. Bristles can be found in dust of beds, which are sometimes in caves, or muddy wallows used by peccary. Scat deposited by these animals dries quickly and is not an important sign.

Wild European hogs are generally black to brown in color, but may be any color due to inbreeding with domestic pigs gone wild. Purebred European hogs attain weights of 300 pounds or more, but many of them are much lighter. Scat of wild pigs resembles "segmented sausage."

Both types of wild pigs root in the soil for roots and nuts, leaving patches of upturned soil. Javelina rootings are much smaller than those of European hogs. Peccary also feed on cactus such as the prickly pear. A photo of feeding sign on cactus by javelina is shown.

Peccary are only found in parts of several states in the southwest and Mexico. Those states are Texas, Arizona, and New Mexico. Wild hogs are primarily found in southern states such as Florida, Georgia, the Carolinas, Tennessee, Alabama, Mississippi, Louisiana, Arkansas, and Missouri. However, populations are also located in California and the Hawaiian Islands.

13

Mammal Sounds

IN THE SAME way a person's eyes can tune them into the presence of wildlife if they know what to look for, their ears can alert them to animals if they know what to listen for. The sounds wildlife make can indicate the immediate presence of animals, whereas by the time visual signs are seen, the animals that made them may be long gone. By following your ears to where wildlife are heard, the animals themselves can sometimes be seen, or at least other signs such as tracks, scat, or feeding signs might be found.

Canines

Friend Buck LeVasseur tells about the time he was camped on the shore of one of Isle Royale's lakes when he heard the distinctive howling of wolves across the lake at dusk. The wolf howl consists of one long note that starts out at its loudest and tapers off in volume. My hound howls similar to wolves whenever he hears a siren. Many large dogs howl in a similar fashion for one reason or another. At any rate, Buck canoed across the lake the following morning and found tracks from the wolves that did the howling.

Coyotes howl differently than wolves. Their calls include a variety of notes. Many times I have heard them start out by barking like a dog, then break into a high-pitched howl that trails off into excited yapping. Groups of coyotes in different locations will frequently vocalize once an initial series of howls has been made. I think coyotes howl for a variety of reasons, but I have heard them most often in the late evening or early morning, probably before and after hunts.

In addition to howls, I have heard coyotes make other sounds, one of which is an uproar of yapping, snapping, and growling. I can recall at least two occasions in the fall on which I heard this type of commotion, and neither time was I able to determine exactly what was responsible for the excitement. There was no snow on the ground either time, and in one case, the sounds came from the opposite side of a river I could not cross. I suspect the animals were either in the process of making a kill or squabbling among themselves over food from a kill that had already been made.

I also heard a coyote bark while trailing what I think was a snowshoe hare. When hunting in pairs or packs I believe that coyotes occasionally ''hound'' game in this fashion while their partner or partners try to ambush the prey. This type of teamwork probably results in some kills that would not have been possible otherwise.

Foxes are the least vocal members of the dog family from my experience. I have heard red foxes make sharp, high-pitched barks several times when detecting my presence. The other foxes reportedly bark in a similar fashion.

Cats

The screams, wails, and moans of wild cats, which are supposed to be very similar to the vocalizations of house cats only on a louder scale, are not heard with the frequency of coyote, fox, or wolf calls. Those who have heard the sounds, which are most often made after dark, told me they were unnerving. I cannot say that I have heard the voice of a bobcat despite spending countless days in habitat they occupy.

Hooved Mammals

Hooved mammals make a variety of sounds, some of which are not often heard. The most commonly heard noises are sounds they make to warn each other of possible danger. Deer and pronghorn antelope make a sound by blowing through their nostrils called snorting or blowing. They normally do this when alarmed, and may blow a number of times before bounding off.

Elk make short, high-pitched barks as warnings. The first time I heard this sound I was stalking a cow with my camera in Colorado when she detected me and barked a number of times before walking off. It seemed like a strange noise coming from such a big animal.

Members of the deer family are most vocal in conjunction with the fall rut. Male whitetails sometimes make low, raspy-sounding grunts either when actually with a doe or when trailing one. This sound cannot be heard very far, but it is distinctive. Once it is heard it is not likely to be forgotten. Spend some time at a zoo with a deer herd in the fall and you should hear the grunting of a buck.

Bull elk make a musical bugle that starts out low and rises in volume to a peak, then falls off again. A number of grunts may be heard at the end of a bugle by a mature bull. Young bulls generally make higher-pitched, squealing bugles than those of dominant animals. Elk calls that imitate bugles can be used to get bulls to respond and sometimes come to the caller.

Bull moose make a grunting sound during their breeding season. Cows are also vocal, making longer, louder bawls. Megaphone-type calls made from birchbark have been used to imitate the calls of a cow moose to get a bull to show himself.

The clashing of antlers together may indicate the site where a pair of bucks or bulls are fighting for the attention of a doe or cow. Butting heads together is a ritual among male wild sheep. Rams customarily square off facing one another, then charge together knocking horns against one another. The resulting sound can be heard for a long distance in the mountains where this ritual takes place. An increasingly popular way of bringing whitetail bucks into view is banging or rattling a pair of shed antlers together.

Does and fawns, cow and calves, ewes and lambs frequently communicate with one another in low calls, but the animals generally have to be close, often within sight, to hear these sounds. Wild sheep make sounds similar to domestic sheep. Last fall I saw a sow black bear and two small cubs at close range, and the sow constantly made a clicking sound similar to what would result from pressing the tongue against the palate then pulling it sharply downward. I assume this was some form of communication with the cubs.

The ankle bones of caribou frequently click as they walk. The combined clicks from a moving herd of these animals can be heard for some distance.

Squirrels

Certain members of the squirrel family can be very vocal at times. Red squirrels, for example, will sometimes chatter and scold a passing person who happens to stop nearby for long minutes. They do the same when seeing other wildlife such as predators. They also call to one another in their characteristic stuttery chatter that begins loud and tapers off in volume. Red squirrels make higher-pitched, chirplike calls in combination with chattering, usually before and after.

The disturbed or warning calls of gray and fox squirrels are generally described as barks, but that description never seemed quite right to me. The call is loud and sharp at first, but trails off in something like a hiccup. The sound is difficult to describe accurately, but once it is heard and identified with a gray or fox squirrel, the call and its association with a squirrel sticks with you. The same is true for any of the wildlife sounds discussed in this book. Once a connection is made between a particular sound and the responsible creature, the animal does not have to be seen to recognize the source of the sound thereafter.

Gray squirrels often wag their bushy tails when disturbed or alarmed and calling. This can be a visual signal of the squirrel's whereabouts when trying to locate the source of the sound. The calls of fox squirrels are usually coarser than those of grays, but sound similar. Chipmunks make a chirping call that can be mistaken for bird sounds. They repeat the same note over and over again, *chock . . . chock . . . chock . . . .*

Marmots, prairie dogs, and pikas can be noisy characters. Marmots make a shrill whistle when alarmed, usually just before heading for their burrow or from their burrow entrance. Woodchucks make a similar warning whistle. Prairie-dog calls closely resemble the bark of a dog, which I am sure is one reason they got the name. These animals will often be standing upright on their hind legs when they bark, and may jump as they bark. One bark from a prairie dog may set off some of its neighbors to bark in response.

The single-noted calls of pikas are commonly heard coming from rocks in mountain ranges of the western United States and Canada. The animals may be calling to one another or announcing the presence of a trespasser. *Enk* comes closer to defining the pika's call than anything else I can come up with.

Pine Marten

Last fall while in Ontario, I heard a low growling sound at one point while walking along a woods road. As luck would have it, the previous winter I was fortunate enough to have photographed the release of a pair of pine martens in Michigan. One of those animals had made sounds I connected immediately with those that came to my ears that moment months later in Canada. I stopped to listen more carefully and heard something rustling in nearby treetops, so I moved closer to investigate, and there was a pine marten looking down at me. The animal twitched its tail and scolded me in much the same manner a red squirrel would, but growling rather than chattering.

As a rule, members of the weasel family are not very vocal, but the pine marten is an example of at least one representative that can be.

Rabbits and Hares

Rabbits and hares are quiet animals when going about their daily routine, but when seriously injured and on the verge of death, they sometimes scream or wail. The sound is high-pitched with one scream often following another until the animal dies. Rabbits killed by predators frequently scream before dying. For this reason, commercial calls that imitate the distress cries of rabbits are manufactured for the purpose of attracting predators to the caller. Predators who hear the sound suspect another predator made a kill and sometimes rush to the sound in an effort to get in on the meal.

I have used calls of this type to bring in red foxes, coyotes, weasels, hawks, crows, and other wildlife. There have been other times I heard the sound made by rabbits that were being attacked. One time when investigating a scream, I flushed a hawk from a snowshoe hare it had just killed. Another time I found evidence of what I believe was the site of an attack of a weasel on a cottontail. The rabbit's cries stopped moments before I reached the spot, my noisy approach probably having scared the weasel enough to enable the rabbit to escape. I found blood, hair, and trampled grass at the spot where the attack took place.

Porcupines

One of the most puzzling mammal sounds I have heard while afield was made by a porcupine. It was early in the fall when their breeding season takes place that I heard a series of high-pitched screams or squalls, nothing like those a rabbit would make. I moved in slowly to investigate and found two porkies, one smaller than the other. The smaller one, which I assume was the female, was making all of the noise. I can only assume she was trying to make it clear to her suitor that she wanted to be left alone. Or perhaps the noise is part of the courtship behavior. I would guess the mating of porcupines has its share of *pointed moments.*

14

Miscellaneous Tracks

Armadillos

The only category I could think of to label armadillos under is miscellaneous. They are so unlike any other animal in North America, and the same goes for their tracks. There are five stubby, long-nailed toes on rear feet and four on the shorter front feet. Toenail marks are usually visible in tracks of all feet because the animals are diggers and their claws are well developed.

Toes on front feet are paired, with the two middle ones noticeably longer than the toes on the outside. There is a distinct *V* formed between the equal-lengthed middle toes. The other two toes are positioned opposite one another on either side of front feet, but those on the inside are slightly shorter than those on the outside. The location of these toes reminds me of the positioning of dew claws on pigs' feet.

On rear feet, the three middle toes are grouped together with two much shorter toes back behind those on either side of the feet. As on front feet, small toes on the inside of hind feet are slightly shorter than those on the outside. The two outside toes of the group of three in front are paired, with a slightly longer toe between them.

The armoured armadillo. (Photograph courtesy of Karl Maslowski.)

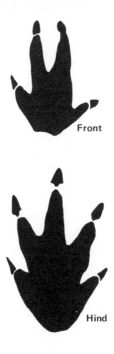

Front

Hind

Armadillo track. (Sketch courtesy of Sue Adams.)

Front feet range in length from a little under 2 inches to a little over. Hind feet are slightly longer. Since the armadillo's legs are short, the animal may drag its tail, partially brushing out tracks when walking in sand.

Armadillos cannot be mistaken for any other animal in appearance. They literally wear a coat of armor and try to curl up for protection when attacked. Their shells have nine bands around them and are brown to gray in color. Armadillos average about the size of domestic cats, weighing up to 17 pounds.

These animals are primarily insect eaters, but also eat lizards, scorpions, eggs, and berries. They sometimes dig in anthills or elsewhere in the ground while feeding and may uproot small trees in the process. Rooting in the ground by armadillos may be confused with that of other animals, so look for tracks to confirm what animal was responsible. Burrows dug by these animals are conical in shape, between 7 and 8 inches in diameter and up to 15 feet in length, but may be much shorter.

Armadillos are presently in the process of extending their range. They are found in states between and including New Mexico and Florida, with Kansas now the northern limit of their range. Like skunks, armadillos are commonly killed by cars on highways, and are considered pests to some degree. Mothballs are an effective repellent.

Mammal tracks and sign are the main focus of this book, but there are signs of other species of wildlife such as turtles, frogs, toads, snakes, lizards, and earthworms that may be encountered while afield as well.

Turtles

Turtle tracks made by aquatic varieties such as snappers and painteds may be seen in the mud along a river or lake during the summer or fall, but they usually only leave the water once a year. Females do anyway, to lay their eggs during late spring or early summer. Sometimes female turtles travel long distances from water to find soft sand where they dig a nest, deposit their eggs and cover them before returning to the water.

Late last spring I was driving along a hard-packed-dirt, woods road that bypassed a lake when I noticed drag marks in the dust made by a painted turtle that entered the road and continued down it the way I was going. The legs of turtles are so short that at least the tail, and sometimes the shell, drag as they walk (see photo). The reptile traveled several hundred yards before stopping to try to dig a nest in the hard packed ground. She didn't have much of a depression dug at that point, so I moved her off to the side of the road where the ground was softer. Eggs laid in a hole in the road would not have much chance of surviving anyway.

A snapping turtle crossing a highway in search of a place to lay its eggs.

Snapping turtle tracks from a display at the Seney National Wildlife Refuge, Michigan.

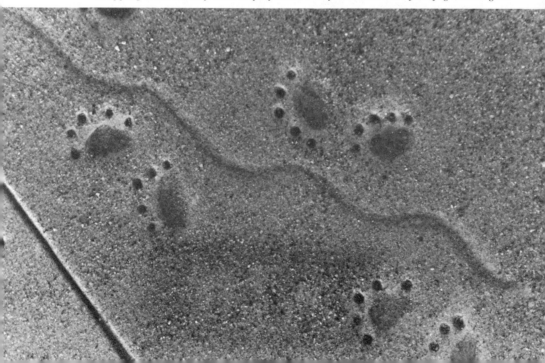

As it is, skunks are good at finding turtle nests. They dig up the eggs and eat their contents. A cluster of broken egg shells on the sand near a lake are the remains of a turtle's nest that a skunk dined on. Turtle egg shells are more leathery than those of birds.

Some snapping turtles attain large size and leave correspondingly wide trails. They sometimes drag their feet in addition to their tails. Turtle toenails are usually fairly long and leave marks at the front of feet, which are round to oval in shape.

In some southern states along the coast such as Florida, South Carolina, Texas, plus desert regions of the southwest, land-dwelling turtles or tortoises live. They dig oval-shaped burrows, wider than they are tall, to fit their shape. These burrows are generally 6 to 8 inches from top to bottom and 9 to 12 inches wide. Tracks leading in or out of burrows should identify the occupants.

Snakes

Snake tracks are easy to identify. Their bodies most often leave continuous, shallow furrows in dust or sand. Furrows are sometimes straight, sometimes wavy, and usually much wider than similar trails left in mud by earthworms. A desert rattlesnake called the *side winder* is an exception to the rule. These snakes make a series of curved diagonal lines as they travel. The ends of these lines are hooked in the direction of travel.

Worms

After a heavy spring or summer rain is the best time to see worm tracks. They come to the surface when the soil is saturated with water and leave slim, linelike trails in the mud along roads and elsewhere. Another worm sign are tiny mounds of irregularly shaped mud on the ground that sometimes form rings around entrances to holes used by worms. Large worms called nightcrawlers appear on the ground's surface at night during spring and summer to mate, usually after or during a rain. Fishermen often use a flashlight to locate 'crawlers and collect them for bait.

Lizards

Lizards are common in arid regions, and their tracks can sometimes be seen in soft sand. Clear footprints may not be visible, just their long, slim toes or scratch marks left by them as they run are visible. Most lizards have long tails, which drag in the sand leaving a line with toe or scratch marks on either side of it.

A worm with part of its linelike trail shown. (Photograph courtesy of Scot Stewart.)

Small, irregularly shaped pile of mud in center of photo was left by a worm where it came to the surface. Numerous mud castings in an area indicate an abundant worm population.

A toad. Notice how right front foot has toes pointed inward as it walks.

Toad tracks in the sand. (Photograph courtesy of Scot Stewart.)

Toads and Frogs

Toads and frogs may also leave tracks in soft mud or dust. Their small front feet with four toes face inward, as a rule. Front toes are shorter and stubbier on toads than frogs. The large hind feet of frogs and toads are webbed for swimming.

Frogs and their tracks are normally never far from water, but toads do not always stay near lakes, ponds, marshes, or creeks and can be seen anywhere. They often make themselves at home in or near gardens where there is grass or brush tall enough to hide in.

The photo of toad tracks shown in this chapter was taken in beach sand of one of the Apostle Islands in Lake Superior. The sand was too hard for footprints to show, but toes on hind feet dug in as the toad hopped, leaving scratch marks. I have seen scratch marks similar to these left by snowshoe hares as they ran along Great Lakes beaches and dirt woods roads.

15

Bird Tracks

UNLIKE MAMMALS, BIRDS only walk on two feet and they normally have four toes on each foot, three facing forward and one back, although the fourth toe does not always show in tracks. The rear toe is usually the shortest of the four.

There are exceptions to this pattern though. The long-tailed, brown, crest-headed roadrunner of the arid southwest is a perfect example. This relatively large predatory bird of cartoon fame that feeds on snakes and lizards, among other things, has two toes forward and two backward. The tracks from one of these birds measured as much as 3 inches in length.

The flicker is another bird with toes that do not fit the normal pattern. There are two toes forward and two backward like the rest of the woodpecker family that flickers belong to. One toe facing each direction is smaller than its mate. Unlike other woodpeckers, I have seen flickers feeding on the ground on a regular basis, so there is a possibility of seeing their tracks. The length of one flicker track along the longest toes was 1¾ inches.

Flickers have prominent red patches on the backs of their heads and are brown on their backs with black-spotted white breasts. A black, biblike marking is on the chest forming the upper margin of the spotting.

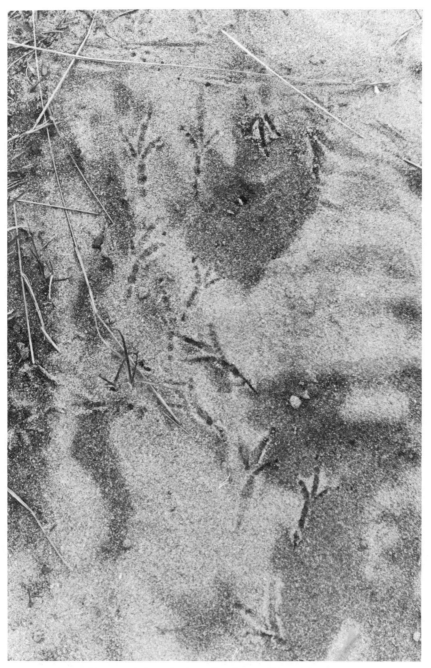

Characteristic paired tracks of a small perching bird.

Getting back to bird tracks in general, there are two basic types of track patterns—hopping and walking. Birds that hop will make tracks with both feet side by side. A series of single tracks, one ahead of the other, are made by walking birds. Birds that spend most of their time perched in trees such as songbirds have a tendency to hop, while birds that spend a lot of time on the ground like quail, grouse, and pheasant walk or run.

For the most part, songbirds leave slim-toed tracks showing four toes, with the rear toe at least as long as the other three. Their tracks measure between 1 and 2 inches in overall length. Quail tracks like the bobwhite and California variety leave prints about 2 inches long, with much thicker toes than songbirds. If the rear toe is visible, it is short and angled off to one side, rather than facing straight back like the footprints of songbirds.

Quail

I remember flushing large coveys of California quail with my father and brother in southern California as a boy. Some coveys contained upwards of fifty birds or more. They occupied brushy valleys and foothills. The males are a blue-gray in color, with large dark patches outlined in white starting under the eyes and covering the throat. Patches of rust coloration are on the lower breast. Males and females have fingerlike top-knots curved forward on their heads. Females are brown in color. Gambel and mountain quail are similar to the California variety. Scaled quail are brown to gray in color with a band of what looks like fish scales on the breast and back of the neck. They also have crests on top of their heads.

The California quail's original range included the southernmost portion of Oregon, most of California and Mexico. They have since been introduced into much of Oregon and parts of Washington, Idaho, Nevada, and Utah. The gambel quail's stronghold is Arizona and adjacent portions of Utah, Nevada, California, New Mexico, and Colorado in arid regions. Mountain quail, as the name implies, are typically found at higher elevations than the other quail in California, Oregon, Washington, and Idaho. Scaled quail inhabit western Texas, most of New Mexico, and nearby portions of Oklahoma, Kansas, Colorado, and Nevada.

Grouse

Grouse tracks are similar to those of quail, but toes are noticeably thicker and longer.* Tracks are between 2 and 3 inches in length. Some of the birds

---

*Pigeon tracks could pass for those of quail or grouse, except the toes are slimmer and the rear toe projects straight back and is longer than those of grouse or quail. The prints of these birds are most common in cities or near barns where they reside. The tracks of a pigeon in the snow in my front yard were 2½ inches long.

Tracks of a ruffed grouse in the snow. Note the short fourth toe angling off to the side and pointing toward the rear.

that fall in this group are ruffed, sharptail, spruce, blue, and ptarmigan. Pheasant tracks are very similar.

The habitat and part of the country where these types of tracks are found are indicative of what species made them, although there is some overlap in the ranges of these birds. *Ruffed grouse* are birds of woodlands and are common in the Great Lakes Region, the eastern United States, and parts of the south, plus states in the northwest. They are also distributed throughout most of Canada and into central Alaska.

As an adaptation for walking in snow, ruffed grouse grow scales along each toe in the fall and shed them in the spring. Tracks of a number of birds can be seen together at times. Ruffed grouse are brown and gray in color with light breasts that have dark bars across them. They got their name from a collar of black feathers usually extended by males when displaying for a female. The rear margin of tail feathers have bands across them producing a continuous band across the tail when it is fanned.

Spruce grouse are found primarily in spruce and jackpine forests. Females are sometimes mistaken for ruffed grouse, being a mottled brown. Males are black. Spruce grouse are also known as "fools hens" due to their habit of letting people approach close enough to kill them with rocks or sticks in some cases. On one occasion I watched Dr. William Robinson, who has studied the birds for years and wrote a book on them aptly titled *Fool Hen*, catch one of these birds by hand, and it was not the first time he had done it.

The distribution of spruce grouse is similar to that of ruffed grouse, except they have a more limited range in the United States (restricted to northernmost states) and is established across a wider area in Canada and Alaska.

Sharptail grouse prefer open country with few trees, although they do spend some time in groves of trees near openings. Flocks of sharptails are common. These birds are tan in color with white breast feathers and short, pointed tails. Both sexes look alike. Their range includes most of the Dakotas, northwest Nebraska, eastern Colorado, eastern Montana, the upper Great Lakes Region, plus much of central Canada and Alaska.

Blue grouse inhabit mountainous regions and the coniferous forests associated with them. The birds are blue-gray in color. They are found primarily in the northwestern United States and Canada, with largest populations in Colorado, Utah, Wyoming, Idaho, Montana, California, Oregon, and Washington. Blue grouse are distributed throughout British Columbia and into the Yukon, plus southwestern Saskatchewan.

Ptarmigan are also mountain grouse, usually living in treeless habitat above timberline or on the tundra, and occur in small flocks. They grow feathers on their feet for the winter. These birds are generally gray to brown in color in the summer and turn white for the winter. Either one of the three

Ptarmigan tracks. (Photograph courtesy of Kent and Donna Dannen.)

species of ptarmigan (rock, willow, and white-tailed) range throughout western and northern Canada and Alaska, and southward in some western states including Washington, Montana, Idaho, Wyoming, Colorado, and New Mexico.

Pheasants

Pheasants are often associated with agricultural areas, with groups of birds present in some fields. Males are colorful, having copper-colored bodies, iridescent blue-green heads, red around each eye, and white rings around their necks. Females are a mottled brown. Both sexes have exceptionally long, pointed tail feathers. Though these birds are now found in a band of states from the northeast to Montana, and in the southern portions of several Canadian provinces (Alberta, Saskatchewan, and British Columbia), they are not native to North America.

Pheasants were introduced here from China many years ago. The band of states the pheasant's range includes in the United States is narrowest in the northeast and is widest at mid-continent, going as far south as the northernmost tip of Texas at that point. Some birds are also distributed in parts of every western state.

Turkeys

Turkey tracks will measure 4 or more inches in overall length in correspondence with their size. Males reach weights of 20 pounds or better while females weigh in the neighborhood of 10 to 15 pounds. To tell the difference between hen and gobbler tracks measure only the length of the middle toe. Those toes are more than 2½ inches on adult toms and less than that for hens. A distance of at least 8 inches separates tracks made by gobblers and the stride of hens is just over 7 inches.

Male turkeys possess beards that grow out of the chest. Wattles, which are normally red, are on the head. The head itself may be red or blue when aroused. Gobblers appear black in color while hens look brown and have naked, dull-colored heads. Hens occasionally grow beards.

Wild turkeys are distributed all across the southern half of the United States from Texas and Oklahoma eastward, with populations established further north in New York, Pennsylvania, Michigan, along the borders of Wisconsin, Minnesota, and Iowa, and in the Dakotas. West of Texas, turkeys are established in parts of Nevada, New Mexico, Arizona, Colorado, Wyoming, Montana, Idaho, Oregon, Washington, and California.

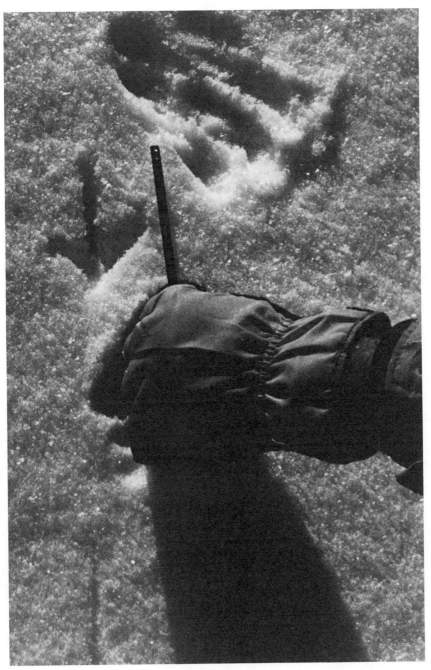

A pheasant track.

Pheasant trail in the snow.

Turkey tracks from several birds. Note the difference in size between those of a smaller hen and a gobbler that are next to each other.

Sandhill Cranes

Tracks of the sandhill crane can be confused with those of turkeys. However, the toes of sandhills are slimmer, have relatively straight edges and are smoother on the underside than turkey toes. Jointed, callous-type pads are on the bottom of turkey feet, and this characteristic sometimes shows in clear prints. Sandhill tracks resemble turkey prints in size, measuring 4 inches or less.

There are two major subspecies of sandhills—*greater* and *lesser*. Greater sandhills are much larger than their relatives. The birds have long legs and are gray to brown in color with the tops of their heads being red. Both males and females look the same. Interestingly, the birds are named after horses with females referred to as mares, males as roans. And, of course, their young are called colts.

Sandhills nest in the upper Great Lakes Region, plus a group of states in the northwest, and most of Canada and Alaska. Since the birds are migratory and winter in the south, they can be seen virtually anywhere. They nest in bogs, but feed in fields, both noncultivated and agricultural.

Great Blue Herons

Great blue herons leave longer tracks than turkeys and sandhills because their fourth toe shows in prints. One track measured between 6 and 7 inches in length. Even without the rear toe, blue heron tracks are distinctive. Two toes on the inside of each foot are close together with a noticeable gap between them, and the toes on the outside.

These migratory birds are blue-gray in color with light-colored breast and head. Long feathers on the chest hang down away from the body and there is a crest or top-knot on the head. Herons are long-legged like cranes. They build colonies of large nests called rookeries in trees over or near water. Blue herons are always associated with water where they feed on fish, frogs, and other items.

Shore Birds

Shore birds such as sandpipers, yellowlegs, and snipe make narrow-toed tracks. Short rear toes may or may not be visible in prints. Small shore-bird tracks are less than an inch long, with those of larger varieties approaching 2 inches. The middle toe is noticeably longer than those on the sides in the tracks of larger shore birds. Their tracks are sometimes abundant in the mud or sand along oceans, lakes, ponds, or rivers. Small round holes left by long, pointed beaks may also be visible where the birds were probing the mud for insects or worms.

Walking tracks of a pair of greater sandhill cranes. One foot is placed practically in line with the other.

A great blue heron track in Nebraska. (Photograph courtesy of Kent and Donna Dannen.)

Woodcock tracks in the mud. Note a couple of holes in the mud where the bird probed with its long bill. (Photograph courtesy of Jim Hammill.)

Woodcock

Woodcock, a bird of the uplands resembling snipe, make similar tracks, only their prints will be visible in the mud of woods roads most often, although they do feed along the shores of rivers and ponds, too. Incidentally, I have seen some snipe in upland habitat with woodcock, so snipe are not "shore-birds" exclusively. Woodcock tracks are about 1¾ inches in length on the average and probing holes may be visible nearby. Snipe tracks may be smaller, measuring about 1½ inches.

Snipe are white and black in color. Woodcock are brown and black, with bulging eyes that are larger than those of snipe well suited for seeing at night. The winter and summer ranges of woodcock encompass the eastern half of the United States and southern Canada. Snipe are distributed throughout North America.

Waterfowl

Web-footed birds include ducks, geese, swans, and gulls. Webbing may not be visible in all tracks though. Only three toes are usually present. Waterfowl tracks usually have marks from toenails visible at the ends of toes. Duck tracks range from less than 2 inches in length for small teal to 3 inches for mallards. The prints of herring gull I measured were 2½ inches long and a glaucous gull left prints measuring a little over 3 inches. One Canada goose track was 3 inches long, but smaller subspecies have duck-size feet. Swan tracks are largest, taping 7 inches or more.

Look for waterfowl tracks in the mud or snow along lakes, ponds, and rivers. However, those are not the only locations where their tracks will appear. Both ducks and geese feed on grain and grass in fields where imprints may be left in mud. I have also seen goose tracks in sand and gravel pits where they have stopped to rest.

Scavengers

Scavengers such as crows, ravens, and magpies make four-toed tracks. The three forward-facing toes of ravens and crows leave impressions closer together than most other bird tracks I have seen. This is because the outside toes face forward more than to the sides like those of other birds. The tracks of magpies are about 2 inches long, with crow prints ranging between 2½ and 3 inches, and raven feet leave prints from 3½ to 4½ inches in length.

Look for their tracks in the sand or snow around the carcasses of dead animals, especially those killed by cars. However, ravens have also clued me in to the locations of both hunter-killed and winter-killed deer. Magpies have long, narrow, black tails with bodies that are black and white. They are seen

Webbed tracks of a mallard duck. They were 3 inches long. (Photograph courtesy of Jim Haveman.)

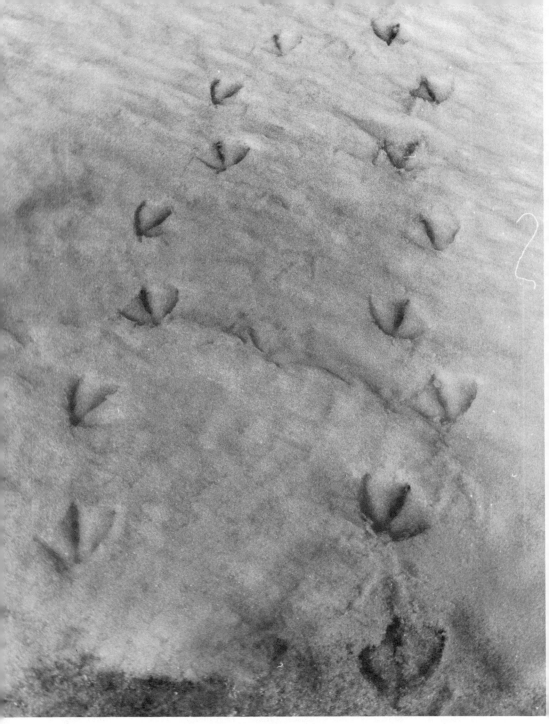

Four-inch tracks left by Canada geese.

Large webbed feet of a mute swan left these 7 to 8 inch prints. (Photograph courtesy of Jim Haveman.)

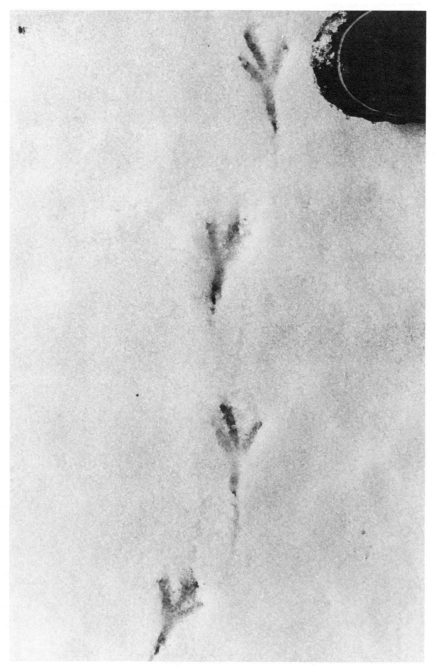

Crow tracks that measured 3 inches in length.

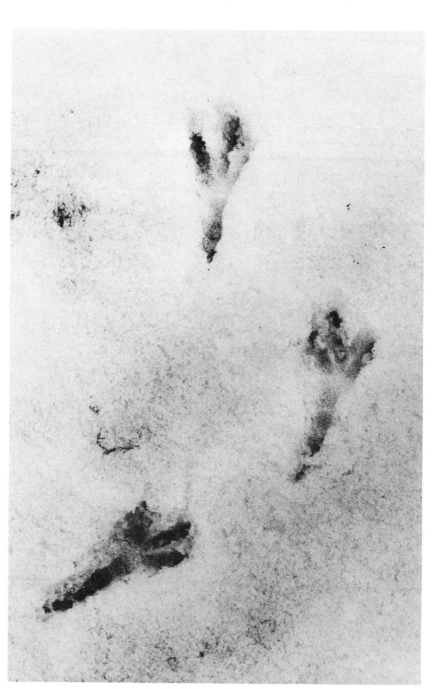

Larger raven tracks.

most often in western North America. Both ravens and crows are totally black, with ravens being the larger of the two. Ravens have slower wingbeats than crows and tails that are more rounded on the corners as opposed to the squared off tails of crows. Ravens are found primarily in the northern United States and into Canada, while crows enjoy a wide distribution in North America.

The only other bird tracks I have seen worthy of mention are those of a bald eagle that was feeding on the carcass of a dead deer along with ravens. The eagle tracks were much larger, with thicker toes and marks from its talons in the snow. Tracks of birds of prey are not often seen, unless associated with a kill, however, there are other signs to look for which will be discussed in the following chapter.

16

Other Bird Signs

WING MARKS ARE another type of track that birds may leave in soft sand or snow. They consist of a series of lines parallel to one another made by vanes in wing feathers. Footprints are often present in combination with wing marks, but not always. When footprints are visible, they can serve as a clue as to what bird made them.

Hawks and owls are least likely to leave footprints where they dive down to the ground to grab prey. When small mammals are the prey, they often gulp them down on the spot and take off again. I watched a great gray owl dive into the snow a number of times one day in an effort to catch mice. The only signs left on the snow were depressions with wing marks on two sides.

When hawks and owls catch larger prey such as rabbits or hares, they may stand on the animal while feeding and take off when full without leaving footprints. I have seen a number of examples of this. So wing marks in sand or snow, sometimes in association with remains of prey, are sure signs a hawk or owl was responsible. It is difficult to impossible to determine which species left the sign, unless a particular bird was seen in the area like the great gray owl I watched. In some cases, wing marks may not even show, but the remains of an animal or bird with no visible tracks from a ground predator present are evidence enough that a winged predator was responsible.

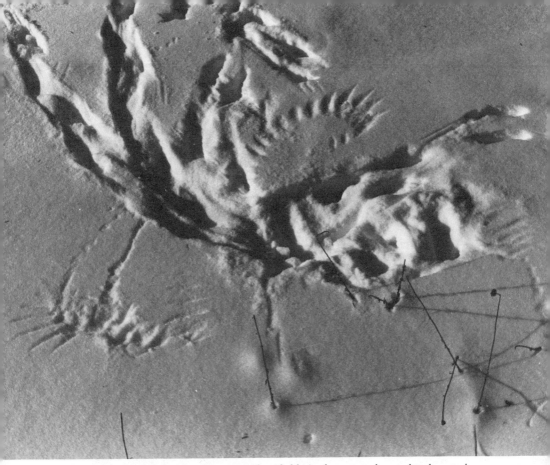

Wing marks and some tracks that are unidentifiable in the snow where a hawk or owl tried to catch prey.

Jim Haveman and I saw just such a situation one time when snow was present. There was a pile of ruffed grouse feathers with no sign whatsoever left by the attacker. An animal as light as a weasel would have left tracks in the snow, so we reasoned a hawk or owl had to have met with hunting success there.

Since I mentioned watching a great gray owl, it is worth adding that these birds represent one of the few exceptions to the normal nocturnal hunting habits of owls. Great grays customarily hunt during hours of daylight. The same is true of short-eared owls.

Another sign typical of hawks, owls, and scavenging birds like magpies and ravens are pellets containing undigestible materials such as hair, feathers, and bones that they ingest with their food. These pellets should not be confused with scats. They are regurgitated, not excreted. Hawk, owl, and raven pellets

Jim Haveman looks in tree for any sign of winged predator that killed ruffed grouse and left no sign in the snow other than a pile of feathers.

An owl pellet consisting of bones and hair regurgitated. This pellet must have come from a big owl due to the size of bones present.

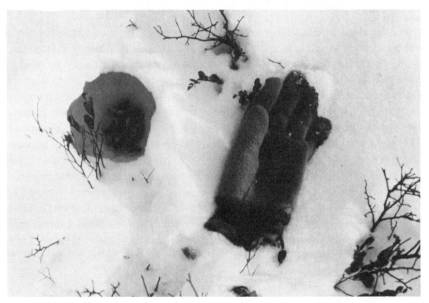

Snow roost used by a ruffed grouse. An accumulation of droppings is present in the bottom. (Photograph courtesy of Jim Hammill.)

are round to oblong in shape most often, ranging in length from 1½ to 4 inches or more.

I noticed a pellet from what I think was a barred owl (because they had been seen in the area) in a rye field last fall. The pellet was lying next to the viscera from a small mammal caught while it was apparently eating rye. Regrettably, I did not record the scene on film because I was anxious to examine the pellet. It contained the hair, bones, and skulls of several small mammals the bird had eaten. At the time, I thought collecting owl pellets would be a good way to obtain cleaned, undamaged, small mammal skulls.

Most hawks and owls nest in trees, but there are some species that live in burrows in the ground that are distributed across the western half of the United States into southern Canada and a portion of Florida. Burrows of owls I saw in South Dakota reminded me of woodchuck holes. These owls may take over burrows made by gophers, armadillos, or turtles. Pellets may be found near the entrances of owl burrows.

The milky white scats of predatory birds are not an important sign, but they may be seen where the birds feed or under trees where they roost or nest. Pellets can often be found under favored roost trees or poles and those that contain nests.

The much smaller white splashings that woodcock droppings consist of may be of interest to woodcock hunters when noticed in aspen or alder thickets. When moist, it is an indication they are fresh, and a woodcock could be nearby.

Grouse scats resemble a dose of toothpaste squeezed from a small tube, but are brown to green in color with one end capped in white. Fresh grouse droppings are a sign that a bird may be nearby. Accumulations of droppings mark roosting or spring display areas. During spring, summer, and fall most grouse roost in trees. When a layer of soft snow 6 inches or more deep covers the ground, they may roost in or under the snow. In the northern part of their range where snow often gets deep, ruffed grouse routinely roost in the snow. The snow insulates them from the cold. The birds may dive directly into the snow or land and wiggle their way into it. When leaving the roost they may walk or fly out creating an exit hole a foot or more from the entrance hole.

Ruffed grouse perform their spring mating ritual—drumming—from logs, although they sometimes use elevated mounds. Scats accumulate on, or next to drumming sites. Photographers who erect blinds within view of drumming logs identified in this fashion may be able to photograph the resident male during his performance. The same is true of other species of grouse if their display grounds can be located.

Another sign that indicates the presence of grouse are shallow depressions in the sand or soil where they dust themselves. Tracks or feathers may be in evidence at dusting areas. The same is true for wild turkeys, which also take

Turkey scat from both a male and female. Gobblers leave relatively straight droppings, while those of hens are often corkscrew shaped.

Dropping from a Canada goose. It measured just over 2½ inches in length.

dust baths. The depressions created by turkeys when dusting themselves are larger than those made by grouse.

Turkey droppings are similar in shape to those of grouse, only much larger. Gobbler scats are normally slightly curved and larger in diameter than the corkscrew-shaped droppings of hens. However, it is not always possible to determine the sex of a turkey by its droppings. Some scats are soft and shapeless. Concentrations of turkey droppings under trees usually mark favored roosts.

When feeding, turkeys scratch leaves behind them to uncover insects and nuts or vegetable matter. Scratchings can indicate the direction of travel of a feeding flock. Leaves pile up behind the birds with the front edge of scratchings pointed in the direction the bird or birds are facing.

Goose droppings are larger yet than those of turkeys, at least for Canadas, averaging over 3 inches in length as opposed to 3 inches or less for relatively straight scats from a gobbler. Scats from geese are straight to slightly curved. Groupings of goose droppings can be found in fields where they have fed or rested.

Wing marks and tracks left by a songbird in the snow as it fed on berries hanging from shrub.

Unmistakable work of a pileated woodpecker on a dead tree.

More holes made by a pileated woodpecker in a live tree.

Duck droppings are not an important sign. One indication of their presence other than tracks, however, are feathers they pluck from themselves while preening. Feathers will be visible on logs or rocks in the water, on the water in quiet sloughs, or on the banks of rivers and shore of lakes where they have rested.

Look to the trees for other signs left by birds. Some woodpeckers such as the yellow-bellied sapsucker and pileated make noticeable holes in trees. The yellow-bellied sapsucker drills a series of holes in the bark of some trees, with birch, maple, and hemlock being preferred species of trees, at least in the Great Lakes states. The holes are usually in several lines parallel to one another and ooze sap that the birds feed on.

Yellow-bellied sapsuckers have white wing stripes that extend from the "shoulder" toward the tail, pale yellow bellies, black crescents on the chest, and red tops on their heads. Males also have red markings on their throats. They nest in tree cavities.

Pileated woodpeckers make holes in trees larger than any other woodpeckers I am familiar with. The holes are either round or rectangular in shape and vary in size, but even the smallest holes are large enough that they seldom escape notice. These woodpeckers dig out the largest cavities on dead trees in an effort to reach insects in the rotting wood. Huge piles of wood chips accumulate under these trees.

Last fall while on a deer stand I watched a pileated woodpecker work on the lower trunk and exposed roots of a large spruce tree at close range. The bird would make several pecks with its beak, sometimes at a sideward angle, then extract a large sliver of wood. After a few minutes of this the bird would stop chopping away and feed on unseen insects, then repeat the process. It was not long before a hole of respectable size was created. The bill of pileated woodpeckers must be strong to endure this kind of activity.

Although these woodpeckers spend most of their time pecking away at trees, they do visit suet at bird feeders. Woody the Woodpecker of cartoon fame must have been patterned after pileated woodpeckers. They have a prominent red top-knot and are black otherwise, except for white markings on the head and neck. These woodpeckers are larger than any other species I have seen and appear to be more common today than they were ten to fifteen years ago. At least I am seeing more of them.

17

Bird Sounds

BIRDS ARE GENERALLY more vocal than most mammals, communicating to one another via calls and other sounds, sometimes over fairly long distances. *The wild turkey* is a good example. Their language consists of a variety of calls that have been carefully studied.

Gobbles produced by male birds are heard more often than any other call because they are the loudest. Toms usually gobble early and late in the day, but gobble most frequently in the spring while in search of mates, or in response to other calls like those made by crows or owls. Gobbles start out loud and trail off in intensity toward the tail end.

Both gobblers and hens yelp, but this is a call most often associated with hens. These calls consist of a number of notes in a rhythmic series, with each note actually being a yelp. A typical series of yelps contains 5 to 7 notes, but may have more. Two or 3 softer purrs or clucks may precede the series that increases in volume. The yelp of a gobbler sounds much coarser than that of a hen. Toms often gobble in response to the yelp of a hen in the spring.

The cackle starts out like a yelp, but has a faster rhythm, is higher pitched, and usually has more notes. Turkeys may use the cackle when flying down from roosts in the morning or flying up to roost in the evening. Hens looking for the immediate attention of a gobbler also cackle sometimes.

The alarm call of wild turkeys is a short, sharp, high-pitched *putt*. The sound is often repeated nervously when a bird or a flock of them is alerted.

Domestic turkeys make the same sounds as their wild relatives and can be listened to for comparison. Wild birds can also be heard in some zoos. A variety of commercial devices that imitate the calls of wild turkeys are available because they are used by people to lure gobblers to them by imitating the calls of hens.

Ruffed grouse make a series of one-noted sounds when disturbed that goes something like, *pete-pete-pete*. . . . This most closely approximates what I have heard countless times while hiking in woods occupied by ruffed grouse. The sound does not carry far, so if you hear it, the bird that you disturbed should be nearby. The pace of the notes varies from fast to slow from one minute to the next, depending on the bird's concern for its safety.

The other sound associated with ruffed grouse that is most commonly heard is made by their wings and is called drumming. Males drum in the spring to attract mates. While standing on a log or some other elevated platform, the birds slowly begin flapping their wings and the pace gradually quickens until reaching a peak, when they stop. The sequence generally lasts 5 to 10 seconds. The performance is usually repeated at regular intervals.

To me, the noise made by drumming grouse resembles a hollow thumping sound. Others have described the sound as being similar to the starting of an engine. The tone is such that some people cannot hear drumming. The noise from drumming does not usually carry far.

Sharptail grouse carry on a more elaborate spring display, involving a group of males that dance about at specific locations called leks, year after year. Leks are most often in openings. When dancing, the birds vibrate their tails, producing a rattling sound, and at the same time, hoot, coo, cluck, and cackle. The sound of a group of males can be heard from a long distance away on quiet mornings, which is when the birds are most active.

Some of the sounds sharptails make are produced by deflating air sacs on their necks. Sage grouse and prairie chickens put on similar displays and make booming sounds with air sacs on their necks. Sharptails cackle when flushed. The sound bears some resemblance to laughter.

Pheasants often cackle when flushed, too, at least roosters do. The sound of the pheasant cackle is completely different than that of sharptails, sounding coarser and deeper in tone. Males crow in the morning much the same as domestic roosters do, only the sound is more abbreviated.

Bobwhite quail named themselves with their characteristic two-note calls. There is sometimes a third whistling note preceding the normal 2 that is written as *ah* or *poor*. So their call would go something like, *bob-white, bob-white, poor-bob-white*, with emphasis on *white* in each call.

California quail make a three-note call written as, *chi-ca-go*, or *cu-ca-*

caw. The call is often repeated and is sometimes preceded by a fourth note, *ut-cu-ca-cow*. Occasionally, I will hear the familiar call from my boyhood on television in the background of a show filmed in California.

Male *woodcock* begin performing their mating ritual at dusk and continue during the night until dawn. They select a spot in an opening near cover and repeat a call that resembles a buzzing telephone, a number of times. Then they fly way up in the air to a certain level, and use a spiraling descent to land where they started, or at least close to it. All during the flight they make a musical twittering sound. It is no wonder woodcock display areas are often referred to as singing grounds.

Snipe put on a high-flying aerial display called *winnowing* during which they make sudden dives that produce high-pitched, pulsating sounds. The whistling noise is produced by their tail feathers. The dives and the corresponding sounds are heard over and over again. I have heard snipe most often during morning hours, sometimes before daylight.

Sandhill cranes make loud, distinctive calls that resemble the noise made by opening and closing a door with rusty hinges. Even so, their call has been described as a type of trumpeting. Great blue herons are not very vocal, occasionally making a hoarse croak.

The enchanting call of *Canada geese* is commonly heard in the spring and fall while flocks of the birds are migrating in *V* formations. Their call is usually referred to as a honk, but there are two notes, *err-onk, err-onk, err-onk*. Snow and blue geese have higher-pitched calls that resemble musical barking.

At least one duck call, the quack, should be familiar to most people. *Mallards* and *black ducks* are the quackers of the duck world, although other species sometimes quack, too. Another sound I associate with ducks is the whistling of their wings as they beat rapidly overhead.

I can also identify the sound made by raven wings as they fly by. The noise can sometimes be mistaken for something running on the ground as a raven approaches because the source of the sound can be difficult to pinpoint until the bird is close. The volume steadily increases the closer the bird gets until it is overhead. The sound is made by air rushing through the birds' wide wings as they fly.

Ravens make a variety of calls from hoarse croaks similar to those of blue herons, to musical warbling. Most people who hear ravens for the first time are usually surprised at their varied vocabulary. When calling to one another, the sound ravens make is a one-noted holler and may be repeated. They also make a fast-paced "wonk-wonk." Crows communicate in caws, which vary in the number of notes used and intensity.

Owls can be very vocal at times, usually in the spring. I have heard barred owls more often than any other. These owls are sometimes referred to as hoot owls because of their calls that go something like, *whoo-whoo-whoo, wh-whoo, to-whoo-ahh*.

These birds of prey, not necessarily barred owls, also make high-pitched screams that sound similar to those a woman might make. I have been startled a number of times by these unexpected calls while in the field after dark. And I knew they were not made by women because I was in locations where I knew there were no other people.

Well, that gives you a general idea of the sounds some birds make. All of the sounds or calls made by each species of bird discussed were not listed. Only the ones that are heard most often were mentioned. Accurately putting bird sounds into words that everyone will understand is difficult. So the best way to become familiar with these sounds, like those mammals make, is to make the connection yourself between a bird and the sounds it makes, and from then on, you will be able to link the sounds with the bird even though it may not be seen.

18

Tracking Wildlife

SO FAR I HAVE discussed how to read wildlife signatures and short sentences associated with their tracks and other sign. Examples of some of the sentences you should be able to interpret, if you have read the preceding pages, in the foot or paw printing of wildlife are simple. "I am a red squirrel." "A black bear ate here." "It is about time the snow stopped. I'm ready to look for something to eat." Now it is time to consider trying to read pages from the diaries of wildlife.

I am being facetious, of course, to make a point. While animals and birds do not keep diaries, they do leave a *daily record of their activities* in sand, mud, and snow by way of their tracks and other sign. The only way to read that record is to follow their tracks. For all practical purposes, snow is necessary to track wildlife. Tracking wildlife in deserts where there are vast expanses of sand might be possible. I am not sure because I have not tried it, but I suspect there are large areas where the soil is too hard for feet and hooves to leave impressions in arid regions.

Unless crusted, snow is soft enough to form tracks made by the lightest, smallest feet. That is the beauty of the solidified form of precipitation. It is a tracker's delight, despite the cold temperatures that sometimes accompany the white stuff. I am fortunate enough to live in an area where snow falls in abundance and, therefore, get a lot of practice tracking wildlife. I enjoy the activity and feel sorry for wildlife enthusiasts who are not exposed to even a few days of snow during the course of a year in which they can examine and follow tracks.

Besides learning what a particular subject has been up to during the course of a day, tracking it gives the tracker an opportunity of seeing it. Failing that, it is not unusual to see other wildlife while trailing one particular animal, sometimes members of the same species. For that reason I always try to carry a 35 mm camera with me while tracking wildlife. A short to medium length telephoto lens (100 to 200 mm) is normally mounted on the camera because they are the most practical. They are lighter, and therefore, easier to hold steady by hand, faster to use and have more light-gathering ability than long lenses.

If there is a lot of snow on trees and brush that will pose a problem by falling on the camera and getting it wet, I may carry the camera in a small backpack. It will not be as accessible as it would be around my neck, but it will be drier, and I am most often able to put it into action just as fast, if not faster, than if snow and water have to be wiped off first. Whether or not the camera goes in back or fanny pack, other items almost always do, including extra film, matches, granola bars or candy, and sometimes a small flashlight plus an extra shirt or sweat shirt. A reliable compass is always in my pocket and a sheath knife on my belt. A tape measure sometimes finds its way into a pocket, too.

Much of the wildlife I track can be long distance travelers such as deer, bear, bobcats, coyotes, and fox. So it is not unusual to follow them for miles. That is why I usually carry a pack. If I set off on the track of an animal that may not go as far, such as a snowshoe hare or a raccoon, sometimes I take a pack, sometimes I do not. However, I always carry a compass. It is less difficult to get turned around and lost when snow is on the ground than when it is not, but with a compass all possibilities of getting lost are eliminated. Carrying a compass has simply developed into a habit with me, and I think it is a good one.

To get the most use out of a compass, take a reading before starting out on a track so you will know which way you are going and which way you will have to come out. This saves having to guess later. If uncertain which way is the correct way to go after trailing an animal, simply turn around and follow your tracks the way you came and they will take you where you started.

On some occasions there is not time to grab extra gear, like the day I was at my car getting ready to go into the woods when a weasel ran across the road nearby. I already had my camera in hand, so I hustled after the animal hoping to be able to photograph it. Within 200 or 300 yards the tracks led to the base of a tree, which the weasel climbed. I got some photos in quite a different setting than I had expected.

One more type of equipment that may be necessary if tracking wildlife in snow a foot or more deep is snowshoes. They will make walking easier. I prefer snowshoes to cross country skis because they offer more support and are easier to maneuver in thick cover.

Tracking small animals such as weasels, rabbits or hares, raccoons and skunks, to name a few, is a perfect way to learn tracking skills. They do not usually travel far, but they do go far enough to give beginning trackers plenty of practice at interpreting what they have been up to. In addition, these animals are abundant enough that their tracks are easy to find, sometimes within walking distance. I started learning tracking skills on snowshoe hares as a boy. There was a two-block section of swamp near my home that I could walk to in a few minutes, and I frequently did. The tracks of some wildlife such as cottontail rabbits, skunks, and squirrels can be found in cities and towns, so woodlots are not necessary to be able to locate all subjects.

Trackers who are interested in the possibility of getting a look at their subject should select the freshest track they can find, either where its trail crosses a road or trail, or by walking into habitat they might occupy and starting to follow tracks once they are seen. Trackers who are not concerned about seeing the animal they decide to follow can pick any track in which the prints are clear enough to identify their maker.

The generally accepted way of tracking wildlife is by following their tracks the way they went. If toes or toenails are visible in prints, they are the best indication of track direction. The way they are pointed is the way their maker is traveling. In respect to birds, some of which have toes pointing both directions, three toes are normally facing forward. A bird like the roadrunner with a pair of toes facing each direction can pose a problem.

However, there is a way to solve the mystery. When walking or running, the birds, as well as animals, usually displace sand or dirt with their feet. As they step or bound forward some sand is normally pulled or pushed in that direction. So loose sand or snow accumulates on the front side of tracks. If toe or claw marks are not visible in the footprints of any wildlife, this bit of advice can come in handy for determining direction of travel.

Another way to determine direction of travel is to look at positioning of the feet. Imprints of rear feet often appear in front of impressions left by front feet, just the opposite of what would seem to be most logical. Rabbit and hare tracks are perfect examples. Since small front feet are at the rear of the larger hind feet in track patterns, the way rear feet are facing can always be determined without seeing toes. The animals are traveling in the direction their hind feet are facing, of course.

Despite the fact that the generally accepted way of tracking wildlife is by following their tracks the way they went, that is certainly not the only way to do it. Trackers who are interested more in where a particular bird or animal has been than where it is going should follow tracks backward. The back track can be as important a part of an animal's daily record as the front track. Backtracking is definitely advisable in situations where trackers do not want to disturb a particular animal, but want to learn something about it.

I have backtracked animals many times. An example comes to mind of one morning when I brought a red fox to me with the help of a predator call. I was curious about how far it had come and what it was doing when it heard the distress cries of a rabbit the call imitated. So I followed its backtrack.

By doing so I learned that the fox came to the call from about a quarter of a mile away, possibly a little farther. The animal ran the entire distance on a fairly direct course. It had been walking when it heard the call, paused briefly to listen, then took off at a trot for me. All of these things were apparent by its tracks.

Getting back to following the tracks of small mammals, the types of things to look for and that are likely to be seen are locations where they have stopped to feed or rest. Rabbits will nibble on twigs and brush and the snow will be packed down where they stood while eating. Droppings should be visible on the packed snow as well as gnawed bark or twigs nipped off neatly at an angle.

Rabbits or hares may feed at two or three locations on different items, then stop and rest. Forms will be shallow depressions where the snow is packed rather than packed flat like at feeding stops. If there are fresh, running tracks leaving the form, the animal heard or saw you coming and left. Prints leaving the form at a casual hop that do not look minutes old were made before you came along. Trackers who move carefully and quietly and know what to look for ahead can sometimes see a resting rabbit before or as it leaves its form.

Rabbit tracks sometimes lead into small, thick patches of brush with definite boundaries that are visible. The animals sometime stop and rest in locations such as this. Rather than follow the tracks into a thicket and making a lot of noise, it is sometimes better to walk quietly around the edge of the cover until the tracks are observed leaving it, where tracking can be resumed. If a complete circle is made around the thicket without seeing the tracks coming out, the animal is inside and can sometimes be spotted by carefully looking. Sometimes a rabbit will exit the way it entered when a tracker is circling the tangle.

The trail of a cottontail may end at the entrance to a burrow, a brushpile, or an old abandoned shack. That is where the animal lives and may only leave its security under the cover of darkness.

One thing I have noticed about rabbits after tracking many of them is they often go in a circle when trailed. It is not unusual to follow a rabbit or hare back to the spot it was jumped. And sometimes they will make the same circle over and over again until the snow is so tracked up the fresher tracks can no longer be followed.

Trackers with partners can use the circling habit of rabbits to their advantage. A person who stays where a rabbit is jumped while his partner follows it has a good chance of seeing the animal, if it does not see him or her first. Remaining quiet and still while waiting for a rabbit to return increases the chances of seeing it.

A major problem encountered when trying to follow the tracks of a particular rabbit is it is sometimes impossible due to an abundance of identical prints left by other rabbits. However, the problem is not as bad immediately after a fresh snow or while it is snowing. What I try to do to avoid this problem when interested in tracking rabbits is to look for relatively small patches of suitable habitat where there are only likely to be a few rabbits rather than many of them.

Raccoons can sometimes be tricky to track, at least when water is not frozen. They frequently leave the snow and walk long distances in the water of creeks, rivers, ponds, and marshes. The only thing to do when this happens is to follow along the edge of the water and look for a spot where the animal leaves it. If no tracks are found in one direction, try the opposite one.

One night I was following the tracks of a larger-than-normal boar 'coon when it crossed a wide, deep river. I followed the bank to a bridge and crossed it to the other bank, then followed that until coming to the animal's tracks again. When he realized I was tailing him, he crossed the river again back to the other side. Some animals do not want to be followed and know how to get rid of trackers.

The tracks of most raccoons end at large trees with cavities in them where the animals usually spend the day. In areas where there are few large trees, raccoons have adapted to living in burrows.

To me, tracking predators such as bobcats, coyotes, and fox is among the most interesting reading of wildlife sign. I seldom return from a day of trailing these animals without feeling respect for them. Their senses are highly developed and their physical endurance is tremendous, both of which are usually revealed in a daily record of their travels.

Part of the reason I respect predators is I feel a kinship with them as a part-time hunter or predator myself. They manage to survive and sometimes thrive by relying solely on their resourcefulness and woodland knowledge. Natural predators do not use tools to secure prey like man does, and man, the predator, is not very efficient in collecting game in many cases even with these aids. What it boils down to, I guess, is I am envious of these animals' abilities, as any tracker or tracker-to-be should be.

At any rate, the types of tales the tracks of predators will tell are often those of hunting success or failure. Their tracks will frequently join those of their prey, usually in running patterns, for short distances. Sometimes the trail of the prey species ends, but often they do not. Actually, predators such as coyotes feed as much on the remains of hunter kills, such as viscera from field dressed deer and the carcasses of winter starved deer, as they do on kills of their own during the fall and winter. It is not unusual to follow their tracks into an apple orchard where they have fed on fallen apples either. Their diet is not composed entirely of meat.

Animals that coyotes kill are usually small, but they do sometimes kill deer. Jim Tembruell and I followed the tracks of a large dog coyote that pulled down a doe late one January. We saw their running tracks together crossing a road, and there was blood from the deer. We followed them from there.

At several points along the trail, patches of deer hide and clumps of hair lay on the snow where the coyote ripped them from the whitetail. The deer ran up small hills or knolls several times. Rather than waste the energy going uphill, the coyote skirted the edges of the hills and intercepted the deer on the downhill side. When the doe plunged down a steep hill leading into a riverbottom, the coyote got a firm hold and hung on. It appeared as though the coyote was dragged by the deer for a while, but the predator apparently got in some telling bites during that time because the partially eaten deer carcass that was still steaming, lay at the bottom of the hill.

Wild predators certainly do not kill as quickly and cleanly as hunters, but they do not have any choice. They kill the only way they know how.

Since most predators are territorial, especially males, their tracks routinely stop at a bush, tree, mound of snow, or some other marker where they lift a leg like dogs do and deposit urine there. These markers are called scent posts. Other predators that pass there will often add their scent to these markers. Trappers sometimes make sets at scent posts, or make their own using bottled scent, for that reason.

Basically, there is nothing complicated about tracking wildlife. It is simply a matter of following the animal or bird's lead, if possible. Sometimes it is not. The procedure is straightforward. Just follow the line of tracks, one ahead of the other.

Where mistakes are commonly made is at points where animals make sudden changes in direction. If a trail has been going in one direction and then seemingly ends, circle around the point where tracks were last seen. If the animal jumped off to the side, the tracks should be encountered while circling. If that does not produce results, follow the tracks backward looking to both sides to see if the animal backtracked and then leaped off to the side. They sometimes do that.

Problems may also be encountered in determining what happened to tracks along roads. Some animals may enter roadways at night or early in the morning and travel along them for some distance before leaving them, sometimes on the same side they entered. Look both ways until the point where the trail resumes is located.

Andy Tingstad and I followed a bobcat one time that walked out on a railroad right-of-way and walked one of the rails for a quarter of a mile or more. We went one direction first without finding further tracks, then the other until discovering where the cat stepped off the rail.

I have followed other wildlife out to roads and could not find any further tracks. What most likely happened in those cases was the animals or birds were hit by cars or shot by hunters who happened to be passing by at the time the animal appeared. These instances occurred at times when hunting seasons were open.

Tracking wildlife is like fitting pieces together in a continuous puzzle. It can be simple or it can be challenging. The tougher the trail, the more satisfaction there is in fitting the pieces together properly.

What it boils down to is anyone who is interested in wildlife is sure to enjoy tracking them in the snow. It is the best way I know to learn about their habits and habitat preferences. Afterall, it's like reading their diaries.

19

Aging Tracks

TRACKS CAN FOOL you when it comes to determining how old they are. I have seen tracks that looked like they were not much more than a day old, but had actually been there closer to a month. Then there have been others that looked much older than they were. This is because aging tracks is subject to a lot of variables, some of which are the medium the tracks are imprinted on, prevailing weather conditions, and the species of wildlife involved. Due to these variables and others, it is sometimes difficult to tell exactly how old certain tracks are, while at other times it can be relatively easy.

Consider sand of various types, mud, clay, and snow as nature's paper. These are the mediums in which wildlife leave their tracks, unknowingly signing their names for those who see them to read. Although, like the signatures of some people that defy reading, the names of some wildlife are hard to read, too.

Most wildlife tracks are not permanent. They can be erased like pencil marks. Nature's erasers are rain, snow, wind, and warm temperatures when considering tracks in snow. From the time tracks are printed, one or more of these factors usually erode prints, sometimes slowly, sometimes amazingly fast, until they are gone. Tracks in mud and clay take longer to erase than those in sand and snow.

Other animals and people can also erase tracks. They generally eliminate prints more quickly than nature does, although not always intentionally. Wildlife tracks printed in sand or snow on roads are perfect examples. The first vehicle driven down the road after tracks are made stamps out some or all of the prints. Wildlife trails serve as their "roads." Each animal that uses a trail may stamp out some or all of the tracks left by animals that used the trail before them.

Heavy rain or snow and strong wind generally eliminate tracks in sand and snow quickly. Rain washes out prints, snow covers them, and wind may do either by blowing loose snow or sand into tracks or actually wisking away the snow or sand prints were in. Tracks under protective pine boughs, canopies of tree limbs, or in thickets are eroded more slowly than those in the open, of course, but even protected prints become weathered and fade quickly under severe weather conditions.

In effect, these conditions wipe the slate clean. Once they pass, few, if any, tracks should remain. As a result, any clearly defined tracks located immediately after severe weather ends are bound to be fresh. In fact, after a storm passes is an excellent time to find tracks of a variety of wildlife, especially if severe weather lasted for a day or more. Animals will go into hiding to avoid those conditions and will be hungry once they are over, so they become very active in an effort to obtain food.

In areas where there is a lack of precipitation such as deserts, the wind may be the primary track eraser. Even so, there are bound to be days on end without wind or precipitation in deserts, as well as anywhere else in North America. These are the times that aging tracks becomes most difficult. Tracks that are at least three or four hours old may look the same or similar to those made a day or two before. Under these conditions, tracks can simply be categorized as fresh or old.

Fresh tracks will show the greatest detail, and when in sand, the soil often appears darker from underlying moisture where it has been disturbed, except in the driest conditions. Tracks in the sand may appear fresh for a matter of minutes or hours, depending on temperature and exposure to sunlight. Prints that are at least a day or two old start to weather and usually look old.

In the snow, fresh tracks are generally clearly defined, except when a thick layer of dry, loosely packed snow is present. This type of snow does not form impressions that are as easy to read as wet snow or layers of the white stuff an inch or less in depth. One reason for this is snow falls into tracks as the animal or bird lifts its feet, partially obliterating prints.

Fresh tracks in the snow will appear fresh for hours, as long as the temperature is below freezing. However, there is a way to get an idea how fresh tracks are by feeling the prints. When animals such as deer walk in

Weathered deer track with uniform colored soil as the surroundings and track details are not as distinct as they were when fresh.

This running deer track may look fresh in mud, but it is not. The mud it is in is frozen, meaning the print was at least made the previous day during the warmest period. Photo was taken early in the morning.

snow, their warm hooves melt the snow under them when making tracks, which leaves the snow soft in the bottom of footprints. That snow gradually freezes and forms ice, depending on the temperature. The colder it is, the faster tracks freeze.

At any rate, tracks that still have compacted snow that is soft to the touch are generally fresher than those that have iced over. Tracks that have been frozen overnight when temperatures usually drop, often form frost in them.

Tracks made in the snow when the temperature is above freezing can be among the easiest to age because they gradually melt away. Wet snow usually forms a perfect mold of the bottoms of wildlife feet. Track features are most distinct when they are made, showing toes, toenails, and sometimes creases or markings on pads themselves. These details fade as the track melts and simply becomes an outline of a foot, then eventually loses all form.

Prints melt relatively slowly when the air temperature is between 35° and 40°F, unless in direct sunlight, and may look fairly distinct for up to three or four hours. I saw a raccoon cross a road one day and took note of the tracks, then returned about ninety minutes later to see how much they melted. The temperature was close to 40°. The tracks started to melt, but their features were still relatively clear at that point. When temperatures reach 45° or more, tracks fade more quickly, seldom looking fresh two hours after they were made.

Tracks in the snow that melt quickly sometimes increase in size or spread out as they fade and become distorted. I have seen the tracks of a big dog resemble those of a bear as a result of this process, and deer tracks take on the proportions of moose prints as they melt, and ordinary human prints transform to those of a bigfoot. So beware when making conclusions about what made tracks that have begun to melt on warm spring days. Melting tracks exposed to the sun often exhibit raised ridges of snow around them.

Aging tracks in the snow is relatively simple during the course of a snowfall. Prints that have no flakes in them are freshest, those with some snow in them are a little older, and tracks that are almost totally covered are the oldest. Even the oldest tracks may only be an hour old during heavy snow. It will take longer for tracks to become covered in light snow showers. A person simply has to use his best judgment when trying to age tracks, depending on prevailing conditions.

It is better to base a judgment on the examination of a number of tracks rather than on one or two. Tracks along snow-covered roads, for example, may have had snow blown in them by passing cars and look old. However, prints a short distance off the road will be unaffected by passing vehicles and may look fresh. The same is true of tracks in fields on windy days. Tracks

Trail of a coyote in the process of melting. Note the raised ridges of snow around each print.

Extremely old tracks in snow. Softer snow around the frozen prints melted leaving raised marks.

in the open will be quickly covered, but those screened by brush will more accurately reflect when they were made and by what.

Be careful when trying to age tracks made in clay, or clay-like mud. Prints made in these materials can become semi-permanent molds, eroding much more slowly than in sand or snow. I remember looking at a deer track in rather permanent mud of a logging road one time and thinking the prints looked fresh. Well, I was by the same spot a month or more later and the track was still there. It did not look any more weathered than it had been before. There is no telling how old that track actually was. One thing for certain about tracks made in mud or clay is that if the material they are in is bone dry, prints are very old.

A person who travels the same route on a daily basis, or at least two or three days in a row, has the best chance of telling how old tracks are regardless of the material they are imprinted on. Tracks that appear one day that were not there the day before are no more than a day old, sometimes less, depending on prevailing weather conditions and the species of animal involved.

Some animals are nocturnal, moving about only at night and others are diurnal, meaning they might be active during either day or night. Then there are other species of wildlife, including most birds except owls, that only move about during hours of daylight. Animals that are diurnal are generally most active early and late in the day, although this varies. And wildlife that is considered to be nocturnal such as raccoons, are sometimes active during hours of daylight.

At any rate, as a general rule, fresh wildlife tracks seen early in the morning were made during the two or three hours before and after daybreak. Trails that appear to be more weathered may have been made during the middle of the night or the preceding evening around nightfall.

The purpose of this chapter is to give some general guidelines that can be used in learning how to age tracks. It is impossible to cover all of the possibilities that may exist. Beyond a basic understanding of aging tracks, proficiency will come from actual experience, anyway. The more you look at tracks under varying conditions, the better you will be able to judge how old they are, not necessarily to the minute or hour, but to the nearest day. In many cases, that will be good enough. And when the conditions are right, the same knowledge will come in handy to make an even more accurate estimation of track age.

It has taken me many years to develop the ability to interpret tracks as accurately as I do today, and I have looked at literally thousands of them over that time. Nonetheless, I still make mistakes or have difficulty reading some prints. The learning never stops. That is what keeps me interested and should serve as an incentive for those of you who want to interpret wildlife's handwriting. It is a language full of discoveries.

Track Aging Field Trip

To further illustrate how to age tracks, a detailed example of how it works may help. A few days before writing the preceding chapter, I took a drive on which the tracks of a variety of wildlife of various ages were noted. The following is an account of how I interpreted what I saw on that drive and how I would have explained it to you if you were with me. Consider it a field trip via words and photos.

The drive is along a snow-covered woods road. We turn south from a main highway to reach it. The calendar says it should be spring, but there is still plenty of snow on the ground to record tracks. The temperature is about 40°F, so some of the snow is melting. Over an inch of snow fell yesterday, covering tracks made up until that time. The snow stopped about midnight, so tracks made after that time should not have any snow in them. They may be partially melted by now though, because of the temperature. It is early afternoon.

"We probably should have come out this morning because wildlife are usually most active at night or during early morning hours, but we'll see what we can find. After a cold, long winter some animals are sometimes active during warming days like today."

As we drive across a bridge over an ice-covered river the first tracks come into view. They are small and follow along the edge of the ice. There are only two footprints visible side by side that are evenly spaced. The animal is obviously hopping or bounding along rather than walking because there would be a continuous line of tracks if it were walking.

"Any idea of what made those tracks?"

"It looks like either a weasel or mink, but the prints are too large for a weasel, so it must be a mink. The fact that they are associated with water is another good clue that a mink was here, but when? Well, the footprints do not have any snow in them because some details of the footprints are clear, so they had to have been made after midnight. Some of the details in the tracks have started to fade, though, due to melting, so the prints weren't made recently either. Since mink are diurnal, being active during either day or night, I would guess these tracks were made about daylight (approximately 7:00 A.M.), give or take an hour, which would make them between five and seven hours old. I'm relatively sure these tracks would have looked fresh if we would have been here at 8:00 A.M. this morning."

Further down the road a big, black bird takes off from the snow to the right side as we approach, and it is correctly identified as a raven.

"Since ravens are scavengers, it was probably feeding on something along the road. Look at all the tracks in the snow where the bird was. There must be something there. Let's stop and look."

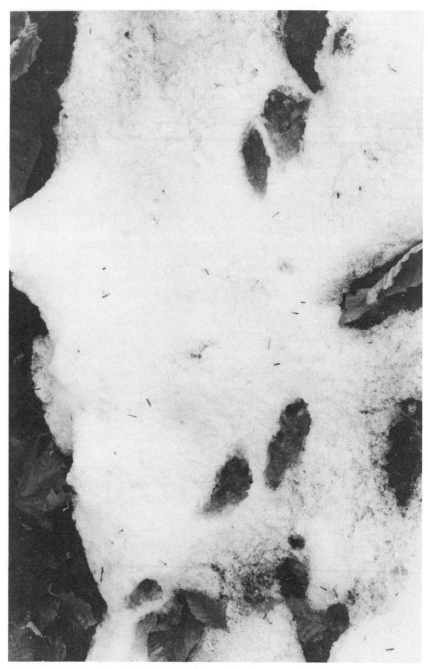

Partially melted mink tracks in snow on river.

A quick look reveals the bird was feeding on a deer carcass, obviously a young animal by its size. Other boot tracks in the snowbank along the shoulder indicate someone else stopped earlier today to investigate as we are doing.

"It's difficult to say how the deer died. Most likely it was hit by a car. Dogs or coyotes, both of which are in the area, sometimes kill deer when they are weak after a long winter, but there is no evidence of their tracks. Even though footprints of dogs or coyotes would have been covered by yesterday's snowfall, the snow is deep enough that outlines of the depressions of their feet would have been still visible.

"At any rate, here are some fresh raven tracks to examine. Notice how distinct many of the footprints are. There are some tracks that are not as clear, too. See them. They were made earlier today and are starting to fade as they melt.

"Ravens roost in trees at night, but they are early risers. Some of these tracks then were probably made shortly after first light, as well as later. There have probably been ravens here other than the one we saw feeding on the deer carcass due to the number of tracks present. These birds frequently call to one another once they find food, so it is not unusual to see a flock of ravens feeding on a deer carcass."

About a half mile from the raven tracks, the snow-covered trail of an animal that crossed the road is visible on the shoulders. Even though footprints themselves are not visible, the oval-shaped steps are obviously those of a member of the dog family, probably a coyote.

"We are too far from homes here for the tracks to have been made by a dog, and notice how the animal crossed directly from one side to the other, not lingering on the road. That is another clue it was a coyote. Since we are in big woods here, it is not likely the tracks were made by a fox.

"The appearance of these tracks confirms my earlier thoughts about the lack of evidence of dog or coyote tracks at the deer carcass. Since these tracks are covered with snow, they were made well before midnight. If they had been made after 11:00 P.M. there would be just a light covering of snow in them. There's about as much snow in these tracks as there is of freshly fallen snow in the road, so they had to have been made before the snow started yesterday.

"Regularly used roads that are routinely plowed are good gauges of how much snow has accumulated since the last snowfall. It started snowing yesterday afternoon, and since coyotes are most active at night, this trail was probably laid down at least the night before last. That makes these tracks more than a day old.

"Well, let's keep going and see what else we can find."

A while later, something appears in the road way ahead in a straight stretch.

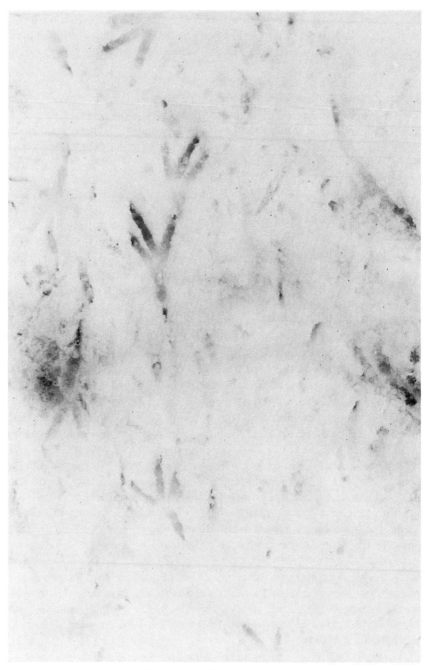

Fresh and old raven tracks.

"Hey, what's that up ahead? It's an animal of some sort, see how it's moving from left to right. Maybe it's a gray squirrel or skunk. Do you see that bushy tail, and how the body is low to the ground? If we're lucky, maybe we can get a closer look at the animal before it disappears in the woods on the right side of the road."

Despite the fact we speed up, the animal is gone before we can get a good look at it. But all we have to do to find out what the animal was is examine the fresh tracks. I stop the vehicle just short of the tracks to avoid running over them.

"Ah ha, it was a skunk. I thought it looked too dark for a gray squirrel, although they are sometimes black like a skunk. It was a striped skunk, of course. That's the only species we have here in Michigan. See how close the tracks are together? Skunks take short steps.

"Let's keep moving, maybe we'll see something else."

The next tracks encountered are those of a snowshoe hare. There is thick swamp on both sides of the road and the hare crossed from one side to the other.

"See how faded these tracks are? They're definitely not fresh like the skunk tracks we just looked at. The prints have definitely melted somewhat, and it looks as though some snow may have fallen in them, too, reducing clarity further.

"If a light covering of snow did fall in these tracks, and I'm fairly sure some did after looking at them more closely, they were probably made between 10:00 P.M. and midnight, maybe a little earlier. Snowshoes are active at night, as well as during the day."

What are all of those little black spots on the snow, you ask.

"Those are snow fleas. They spend most of the winter under the bark of trees, and on days like today when the temperature gets above freezing they start appearing on the snow, sometimes in big bunches that make the snow look dirty. Even though they are called fleas, they aren't parasites like those on dogs, cats, and other pets. They feed on decaying vegetable matter primarily. One thing they do have in common with the parasites is that they hop from one spot to another. Watch them closely, and you'll see what I mean."

After watching snow fleas for a short time, we continue on. We don't have far to go before the outing is over. As luck would have it, we manage to see another animal cross the road ahead of us. I did at least. You were busy looking off to the side of the road for tracks when the animal ran across the road well ahead of us. You got to see the fresh tracks though.

The animal was far enough away that it was difficult to accurately identify it, but it looked black so I thought it might have been another skunk. We stopped at the tracks to find out what the animal was.

Fresh skunk tracks climbing snowbank along woods road.

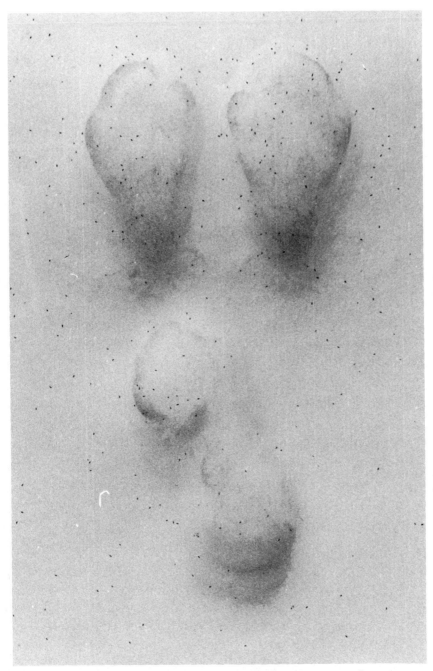

Snowshoe hare track with snow in it. Black spots are snow fleas.

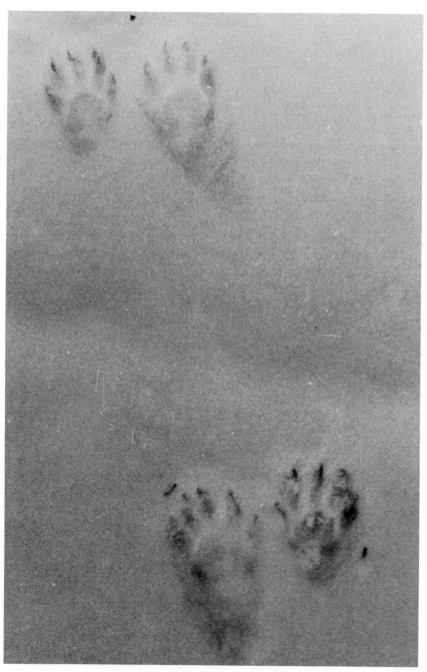

Fresh tracks of a raccoon crossing the road.

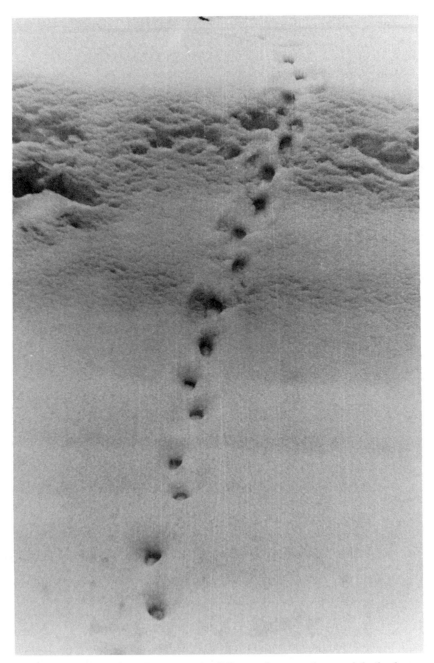

Partially melted skunk tracks. Notice the difference between these and the fresh ones. Claw marks are not visible.

"Well, whatta you know. It wasn't a skunk afterall. That long hind foot and handlike front foot next to each other say it was a raccoon. I'll bet it's a male wandering around looking for a mate. They breed at this time of year. Raccoons are normally nocturnal, but it's not unusual for them to move about during daylight hours in the spring when searching for a mate. It's 2:30 now, which is even a little early. They normally wait until evening before beginning to move about.

"Being able to identify wildlife tracks has sure proved to be an advantage on this trip. We saw two animals, neither of which was close enough to identify positively on sight. We could have guessed at what they were, of course, like some people do, and might have been right, but with our track reading skills, there was no need to guess.

"Not much farther to go now before we get back to the highway and the end of our ride."

A half-mile farther we turn north, back toward the highway, but before we reach it we come to another set of tracks crossing the road. Each print is close together, one ahead of the other, like the trail of an animal we saw earlier. Another skunk was on the move. It cannot be the same one because we are at least five miles from where we saw the one cross the road, and they do not travel anywhere near that distance in a day, as a rule.

"See how different this track looks than the other one? It has melted enough to eliminate the toes, leaving oval holes in the snow. There's no snow in the tracks, so they were made after midnight, but I think they are much fresher than that. Some of the faded raven tracks back there looked older than this track, so that's a good indication these prints were made sometime after daylight.

"This skunk probably left its burrow when the temperature warmed sometime late this morning rather than before daylight. I'd say this track was made four or five hours ago, possibly even three."

Well, I hope you enjoyed the trip and learned a little bit about aging tracks, as well as a few things you might not have expected. Whenever you expect to go afield the following day to look at tracks, try to take note of when the rain or snow stops, or the wind lets up. If snow is involved, consider using the amount that fell on your porch or vehicle as a gauge of the accumulation since the snow started. If you think of it, make a footprint in the snow before going to bed. The condition that print is in the morning can serve as a gauge of how old wildlife tracks that are encountered might be.

Tracks that look older than your footprint were made before you turned in. Those that look fresher were made afterward, and so on. If you want to know when wind, snow, or rain stopped and do not want to stay up all night to find out, the local weather bureau may be able to provide that information.

20

Taking Tracks Home

FOR ONE REASON or another, outdoor enthusiasts may want to take tracks that they find home with them, especially those of rare or unusual wildlife. Or maybe it will be the prints of a common species that are exceptionally large or unique in some way that trackers will want to preserve. Whatever the case may be, there are a number of ways of preserving tracks.

Photography

One of the simplest ways of doing this, in my opinion, is preserving an image of the footprint or prints on film, examples of which are found throughout this book. Individual tracks, groups of prints, and walking, hopping, or running track patterns can all be recorded in a very few minutes with little effort. Single lens reflex (SLR) 35 mm cameras are best suited for recording tracks on film, but range-finder models in the same format will also do.

SLR 35 mm cameras are designed so that the photographer looks directly through the lens to determine exactly what he or she wants in the photograph. Another advantage of SLR cameras is they can be fitted with interchangeable lenses to increase or decrease the field of view in a photograph. Wide-angle lenses increase the field of view and make objects appear further away. Telephoto lenses decrease the field of view and magnify subjects, making them appear closer.

Most SLR cameras come equipped with "normal" lenses of 50 mm, which are the equivalent of one power. In other words, scenes viewed through normal lenses appear as they would to the human eye. Lenses with greater magnification than 50 mm are telephotos, and those less than normal are wide angles.

Either normal or wide-angle lenses are well suited for photographing tracks. Normal lenses do the best job on individual tracks or groupings of several, but are also satisfactory for recording walking or running trails of wildlife. However, wide-angle lenses capture these best.

Range-finder 35 mm cameras differ from SLRs in that the viewfinder and lens are offset, so photographers usually see more area than actually registers on the film. Markers in viewfinders normally outline the scene that will appear on processed film. One disadvantage of range-finder cameras is they are not designed for changing lenses. They often come with wide-angle lenses, although not by much. The first 35 mm camera I owned was made by Canon and came equipped with a 40 mm lens, but there may be variations from one manufacturer to another. Something worth considering for those interested in purchasing a camera is that range finders are generally cheaper than SLRs.

Many 35 mm cameras available today have automatic features making them easy to use. However, even manual models can be mastered in a short time. All of the numbers and dials on 35 mm cameras scare some people, but only three simple adjustments have to be made to take a picture—adjust lighting, select a shutter speed, and focus. Focusing is the only step required on some automatic cameras, and that may not even be necessary on cameras of the future.

Instruction manuals that come with cameras explain how to use them, so I will not get into that, but there are some special considerations necessary to obtain good photos of tracks that will be discussed. When photographing tracks, depth of field (the amount of area that is in focus in a photo) is important. The shorter the distance from the camera to the track, the less depth of field there will be and the same is true when wide lens openings are used. The bigger the opening, the less depth of field there will be. In other words, the largest lens opening gives the least depth of field, and the smallest yields a photo with the largest area possible in focus.

Since the tracks of some animals such as deer are pressed into sand, mud, or snow creating depressions varying in depth, it is important that the entire area be in focus to get the best results. To achieve this, photograph tracks with the slowest shutter speed possible, which yields the smallest lens opening possible, and without getting any closer than necessary.

Most people can take good photos by hand holding a camera with a normal lens at a shutter speed of 125th of a second (simply 125 on most shutter-speed selectors). Many can do it at one-sixtieth or one-thirtieth of a second. However, people who tend to be shaky will get better photos with shutter speeds of at least 1/250th of a second.

If several tracks are relatively close together and show detail, it is best to include them all in a photo rather than homing in on one footprint. However, if there is enough light enabling you to use the smallest opening on your lens, or at least close to it, there should be no problem moving in as close as possible to photograph a single print. Most normal lenses do not focus much closer than 2 feet, but specialized macro lenses of various magnifications enable focusing at closer distances. The smallest lens opening should always be used when photographing a line of tracks, so many of them will be in focus.

The type of film used will have some bearing on what lens openings and shutter speeds will be available to you. High speed films are most sensitive to light, enabling photographers to use the smallest lens opening possible under prevailing light conditions. This type of film is most useful in situations where lighting is usually not bright. In bright situations where there is plenty of light, slower speed films are adequate. Slow films have less grain, and therefore better quality than fast films, especially when enlargements are made from negatives or slides.

Film speeds are rated according to ASA numbers. Films with ASAs of 400 are considered fast. Moderate speed films have ASAs of 100 to 200. Slow films are rated at less than 100.

Under exceptionally bright conditions such as exist on sunny days when snow is present, there can be too much light to properly expose high speed film. However, there is a way to get around that. A polaroid filter, which can be obtained to fit on camera lenses, reduces the amount of light reaching the film, enabling photographers using high speed film to get proper exposures. Other types of filters have a similar effect, but polaroids are the best I have found for this purpose. A filter would not be necessary, of course, if a slow film is used under bright light conditions.

Sunny days are the best for photographing tracks in the snow, by the way. The light creates shadows in prints, which gives them depth, and highlights details. Photos of tracks taken on cloudy days are generally of poorer quality than those exposed in the sun for that reason.

Properly exposing tracks in the snow can be a problem because most light meters read the much brighter snow around them. To correct for this,

I generally take a photo or two at the setting my meter says, then I open the shutter one stop and take a couple more. The process is repeated one more time before I am satisfied. Sometimes I even underexpose, according to my meter, a couple of photos to make sure I will have at least two properly exposed photos. The photos that are overexposed according to my meter often turn out best.

A flash unit is the answer for photographing tracks under low light conditions. It is best not to use high speed film in conjunction with a flash because most photos taken at short distances will be overexposed. Many people believe it has to be dark before a flash is necessary. That is not true if quality photos are desired. Once the light fades enough that it becomes necessary to use moderate to large lens openings, a flash will enable you to use small lens openings to achieve maximum depth of field.

When focusing on individual tracks, I always focus on the bottom of the footprint. The entire track will be in focus though if there is enough depth of field. Best results are achieved when photographing a line of tracks by focusing on a print a third of the way along the trail, so two-thirds of the tracks are beyond the point of focus and one-third behind it.

One other point to remember about photographing tracks if you are interested in showing their size is to put something next to prints that will show scale. Any number of objects can be used such as coins, pens, lens caps, knives, tape measures, or anything else of known size. Natural objects such as leaves, acorns or flowers generally detract less from a photo than the other items mentioned, but sometimes natural objects are not readily available. Sometimes parts of the anatomy like a hand or foot, either yours or someone else's, work well to show scale.

If you consider yourself more of an artist than a photographer, tracks can be sketched in a pocket notebook or on a piece of paper. Appropriate dimensions can be noted on the sketch. If you do not have a tape measure, remember a dollar bill measures 6 by 2½ inches, although bills are not precise enough for many measurements. What I sometimes do when I want to measure a track and do not have a measuring device is break a twig to correspond with the track size and measure the twig when I get home.

Making Casts

A more precise way of preserving tracks to bring home is to make plaster casts of them. Simply mix dry plaster with water in a can or other container, pour into the selected track or tracks and let dry. Once the plaster is dry, use a knife to pry the cast free. Loose dirt clinging to the cast can be brushed off in the field and the rest removed later.

Ideally, a piece of heavy paper or an aluminum sleeve should be placed

Before beginning to make a plaster cast, make sure to select a track representative of the particular animal.

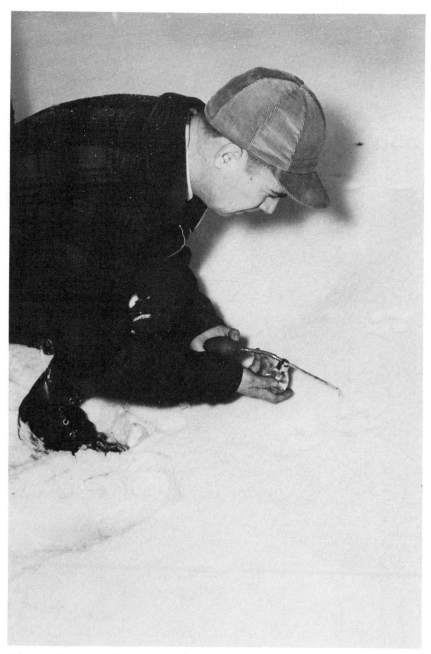

After deciding on a print, spray it with water. This will freeze the surface and strengthen the track before receiving the plaster.

Use a piece of metal edging to form a collar around the track and pour the plaster, the consistency of pancake batter, into the track until it completely covers the surface.

After the plaster hardens, remove the collar and pick up your mold. You are now ready to return home and complete the next step.

This time take a square form and fill it with plaster first.

Take your field mold and place it on top, bottom side down. In other words, have it in the same position as when you picked it up in the field.

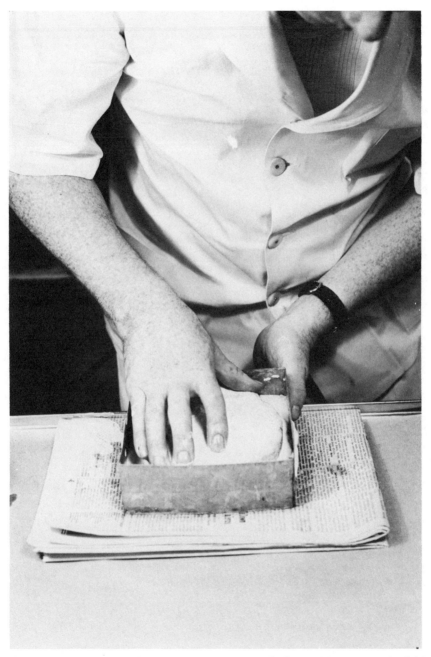

Press down enough to make an impression on the soft plaster. Then remove the field mold and allow the new mold to dry.

When the plaster is dry, remove the square form and you have your preserved animal track.

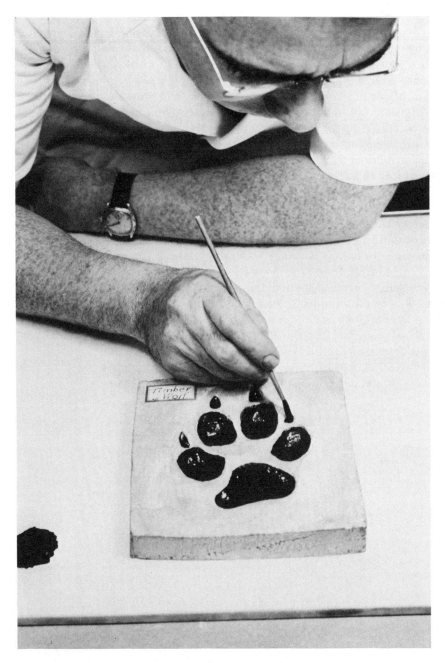

To add distinction, the track can be labeled and painted with any craft paint available in most variety stores or craft shops.

around a track before pouring the plaster, to contain the liquidy substance. However, this is not absolutely necessary, especially when working on level ground. When on a slope, soil, rocks, or pieces of wood can be used to form a ring around the track, at least on the downhill side.

Making casts of tracks in the snow can be a problem at times because the plaster may melt the snow, deforming or eliminating the print that was to be preserved. One way to get around this is to first spray the track with water, which forms ice and reinforces the print. The temperature has to be below freezing for this to work, of course. When the plaster is mixed it is a good idea to add snow to the mixture to keep it cold.

A sequence of photos in this chapter from the Wisconsin Department of Natural Resources shows step by step how to make plaster casts of tracks in the snow. And the sequence continues by illustrating how to make plaster casts of tracks the way they originally appeared in the snow. The added step necessary to do this is simply by making a cast of a cast.

The original cast exhibits the track in a raised position. Once it is cleaned, a container large enough to fit the cast in is filled with plaster, and the raised track is pressed into the second mold before it dries. The second cast shows a print that looks as if the animal itself stepped there. Finished casts are then painted and photographed. Photos of some tracks prepared in this fashion appear on the pages of this book.

Natural casts of tracks can sometimes be found in dried mud, and with some careful digging, can be salvaged intact to take home.

Tracking Quiz

Answer the following questions true or false.

		True	False
1.	Since mule deer are generally larger than whitetail deer, it is almost always possible to tell their tracks apart.	_____	_____
2.	All members of the deer family rub their antlers on trees, but only whitetail deer make a network of scrapes for breeding purposes.	_____	_____
3.	The shape of turkey scat can be used to determine the bird's sex.	_____	_____
4.	Turkey tracks resemble those of the great blue heron.	_____	_____
5.	Rabbits and hares have five toes on their hind feet, while tree squirrels have four.	_____	_____
6.	Only the hind feet of otters are webbed, and the webbing always shows in tracks.	_____	_____

		True	False
7.	Porcupines have five toes on their hind feet, but only four on front feet.	_____	_____
8.	Rabbit and hare tracks are shaped roughly like a triangle.	_____	_____
9.	The front feet of animals always leave imprints ahead of rear feet, as would be expected.	_____	_____
10.	Marks from dew claws register in the tracks of javelina as often as they do in prints of European wild hogs.	_____	_____
11.	Claw marks of the black bear are not as prominent in their tracks as they are in the tracks of grizzly bears.	_____	_____
12.	The tracks of lynx are sometimes bigger than those of mountain lions even though mountain lions themselves are much bigger.	_____	_____
13.	Pads on the feet of red fox do not always show clearly in tracks during the winter because they are covered with hair.	_____	_____
14.	Red fox have longer toenails than gray fox because they sometimes use them for climbing trees.	_____	_____
15.	Claw marks always register in the five-toed tracks of bobcats.	_____	_____
16.	Armadillo tracks can be difficult to distinguish from those of opossums at times.	_____	_____
17.	Gophers often plug the entrances to their burrows.	_____	_____
18.	Star-nosed moles leave tracks that resemble stars, and that is partly how they got their name.	_____	_____
19.	Weasels usually only leave two marks in soft snow where they travel, and sometimes they travel underneath the snow rather than on top.	_____	_____
20.	Any camera will take great photos of animal tracks.	_____	_____
21.	Depth of field is how far tracks sink into sand, mud, or snow.	_____	_____

		True	False
22.	It is impossible to photograph tracks in the snow on sunny days using high speed film.	_____	_____
23.	When aging tracks it is helpful to know when it snowed or rained last.	_____	_____
24.	Animals always kick sand and snow behind them when walking.	_____	_____
25.	Wildlife tracks are not likely to be seen in cities or towns, so it is necessary to go on a field trip to find them.	_____	_____
26.	The difference between fresh and old tracks can sometimes be determined by feeling them.	_____	_____
27.	The only way to learn anything about wildlife when tracking them is to follow them the way they are going.	_____	_____
28.	All bird tracks have three toes facing forward and one toward the rear.	_____	_____
29.	Sandhill crane tracks look similar to those of turkeys.	_____	_____
30.	Beaver tracks are always easy to find near water where they have been working.	_____	_____
31.	The tracks of some members of the weasel family may end at the base of trees just like those of squirrels.	_____	_____

Answers to True and False questions.

1. False. The only time their tracks can be reliably distinguished is when running prints are visible.

2. True.

3. True.

4. False. Herons have four toes in tracks, turkeys three.

5. False. The other way around.

6. False. All feet are webbed, although front ones do not have webbing as prominent as the rear. Even on rear feet webbing does not always appear in tracks.

7. True.

8. True.

9. False. The other way around.

10. False. Dew claws seldom show in javelina tracks.

11. True.

12. True.

13. True.

14. False. Gray foxes are the tree climbers.

15. False. Bobcats have four toes and their claws are sheathed.

16. False. Tracks of both of these animals are distinctive.

17. True.

18. False. Moles of any type seldom leave tracks, but they do leave visible tunnels. These animals do not walk on their noses.

19. True.

20. False. Thirty-five mm cameras give the best results.

21. False. It is the area that is in focus in finished photo.

22. False. Use a polaroid filter.

23. True.

24. False. They pull or push sand and snow forward.

25. False. Many birds and some mammals are common in cities.
26. True.
27. False. Backtracking can be as enlightening.
28. False. Some have two forward and two backward.
29. True.
30. False. Beaver tails frequently brush out tracks.
31. True.

Bibliography

Bull, John, and Farrand, John, Jr. *The Audubon Society Field Guide to North American Birds*. New York: Alfred A. Knopf, 1977.

Bump, Gardiner; Darrow, Robert W.; Edminster, Frank C.; and Crissey, Walter F. *The Ruffed Grouse*. Harrisburg, Pa.: Telegraph Press, 1947.

Burt, William H. *Mammals of the Great Lakes Region*. Ann Arbor: University of Michigan Press, 1957.

Burt, William H., and Grossenheider, R. P. *A Field Guide to the Mammals*. Cambridge, Mass.: Riverside Press, 1952.

Chase, Myron. *Field Guide to Tracks of North American Wildlife*. Fort Atkinson, Wis.: Nasco, 1969.

Dalrymple, Byron W. *North American Game Animals*. New York: Crown, 1978.

Guthery, Fred. "Footprint Measurements of Canadian Sandhill Cranes." *Journal of Wildlife Management* 39: [1975]: 447.

Johnsgard, Paul A. *Grouse and Quails of North America*. Lincoln, Neb: University of Nebraska, 1973.

Lampe, David. "Unloved and Unloving, the Armadillo Blunders On." *National Wildlife Magazine*, February/March 1977, p. 34.

Leopold, Starker A.; Gutierrez, Ralph J.; and Bronson, Michael T. *North American Game Birds and Mammals*. New York: Charles Scribner's Sons, 1981.

Mason, George. *Animal Tracks*. New York: William Morrow and Co., 1943.

McCullough, Dale R. "Sex Characteristics of Black-Tailed Deer Hooves." *Journal of Wildlife Management* 29: [1965]: 210.

Mathews, F. Schuyler. *Field Book of Wild Birds and Their Music*. 2d ed. New York: Knickerbocker Press, 1921.

Murie, Alaus J. *A Field Guide to Animal Tracks*. 2d rev. ed. Boston: Houghton Mifflin Co., 1974.

Rue, Leonard Lee III. *Complete Guide to Game Animals*. 2d rev. ed. New York: Van Nostrand Reinhold Co., 1981.

―――. *The Deer of North America*. New York: Crown, 1978.

―――. *Furbearing Animals of North America*. New York: Crown, 1981.

Smith, Richard P. *Deer Hunting*. Harrisburg, Pa.: Stackpole Books, 1978.

Webster, David. *Track Watching*. New York: Franklin Watts, 1972.

Williams, Lovett E., Jr. *The Book of the Wild Turkey*. Tulsa, Okla.: Winchester Press, 1981.

Wootters, John. *Hunting Trophy Deer*. New York: Winchester Press, 1977.

Index